Best Places to Bird in British Columbia

Local experts / Insider knowledge / Specialty birds

Russell Cannings
& Richard Cannings

BEST PLACES
TO BIRD

— IN —

BRITISH COLUMBIA

GREYSTONE BOOKS

Vancouver/Berkeley

Greystone Books Ltd.
www.greystonebooks.com

Cataloguing data available from Library and Archives Canada
ISBN 978-1-77164-166-1 (pbk.)
ISBN 978-1-77164-153-1 (epub)

Editing by Lesley Cameron
Proofreading by Stefania Alexandru
Cover design by Nayeli Jimenez and Peter Cocking
Interior design by Naomi MacDougall
Cover photograph by Liron Gertsman
Photographs by Joshua Brown (page 140), Richard Cannings (pages 112, 160), Russell Cannings (pages 5, 198), Wendy Coomber (page 186), Gordon Curry (page 13), Liron Gertsman (pages 16, 22, 36, 42, 50, 102, 108, 116, 130, 146, 152, 156, 164, 176, 182, 190), Melissa Hafting (pages 74, 88, 94), Robin Horn (pages ii [top], 32), Logan Lalonde (pages ii [bottom], 124), Ilya Povalyaev (pages 8, 28, 58, 62, 66, 80, 134, 194), Patricia Taylor (page 46), Murphy Shewchuck (pages 84, 174), Liam Singh (pages xii, 170)
Maps by James Bradley

Printed and bound on ancient-forest-friendly paper in China by 1010 Printing International Ltd.

We gratefully acknowledge the support of the Canada Council for the Arts, the British Columbia Arts Council, the Province of British Columbia through the Book Publishing Tax Credit, and the Government of Canada for our publishing activities.

Canadä

Photos on previous spread:
TOP: Sandhill Cranes, Reifel Refuge. ROBIN HORN

BOTTOM: Sage Thrasher, White Lake. LOGAN LALONDE

To all our birding friends around the province.

Without your knowledge, openness, and support,
books like this would not be possible.

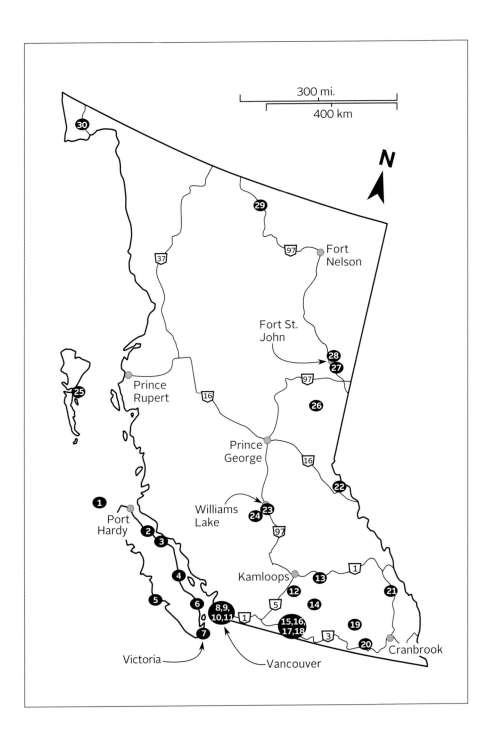

CONTENTS

INTRODUCTION

WHEN I WAS first approached about writing a guide to the thirty best places to bird in British Columbia I had two main concerns: It sounded dangerously similar to my first book—*Birdfinding in British Columbia*—and I knew I couldn't possibly come up with a Top 30 without leaving out several hundred equally magnificent places and consequently upsetting dozens of people as a result. However, I couldn't resist the temptation to write more about my home province and the phenomenal birding areas therein.

To address my first concern, I have tried my best to update, improve, and add to the information contained in my first book, including more site-specific information. I'm also sharing a few stories and musings that I hope enhance the context of each chapter. I know that several fantastic birding locations were left out, and certainly Powell River,

Kitimat, the Stewart-Cassiar Hwy., and many lovely areas in central and southeastern British Columbia deserve more attention, but those give me an excuse for a future book.

Did I have a strict formula for selecting the sites in this book? Not really. In general, I wanted each major ecological region of BC to be represented, but I also had to keep in mind where most birders are, where most birders travel, and what sites provide a variety of birds in settings that are both beautiful and convenient. So why did I include Triangle Island? Quite frankly, it's easily one of the most important locations for birds in BC. Unfortunately, it's also one of the hardest places to get to in the province, but its remoteness creates an allure and mystique that makes it all the more interesting to read about. After Triangle Island, the chapters are ordered in the same way one might explore the province by car, with each site connected to the next by one of BC's numerous highways (though ferries and small side-trips are, of course, necessary for some). Fittingly, the journey ends in another remote triangle—that of the Haines Triangle.

Some birding sites demand attention due to the sheer beefiness of their checklists, while others offer unique species in beautiful environments. My own experience presents an obvious bias. You'll notice that four Okanagan Valley sites are included. However, personal experience brings an enhanced understanding of an area, and I hope readers will appreciate the personal touch in each chapter along with practical information about finding birds. Each chapter has an overview, a birding guide to both the birds and how best to see them, and directions on getting to the sites.

FINDING THE BIRDS

Before you set out, consider creating an account for free at eBird.org, a worldwide public database for registering bird sightings, to find out where your target birds have been seen most recently.

BIRDING ETHICS

Anyone who gets enjoyment from birds cares about them in some way, so it seems reasonable that we should take steps to ensure that our activities have a minimal impact on their habitats. The American Birding Association has a Code of Birding Ethics (http://listing.aba.org/ethics) that is quite suitable for birding pursuits around the world. Much of it is common sense, but I think it's important to emphasize the following:

1(b) To avoid stressing birds or exposing them to danger, exercise restraint and caution during observation, photography, sound recording, or filming.

Limit the use of recordings and other methods of attracting birds, and never use such methods in heavily birded areas, or for attracting any species that is Threatened, Endangered, or of Special Concern, or is rare in your local area;

Keep well back from nests and nesting colonies, roosts, display areas, and important feeding sites. In such sensitive areas, if there is a need for extended observation, photography, filming, or recording, try to use a blind or hide, and take advantage of natural cover.

Use artificial light sparingly for filming or photography, especially for close-ups.

And with that, let me wish you happy birding.

The Tufted Puffin is surely one of the most striking birds in Canada, and yet few birders ever see them due to their preference for foraging offshore and nesting on remote islands like Triangle. LIAM SINGH

—1—

TRIANGLE ISLAND

THE HMCS *Vector* departed Port Hardy on a warm August evening. I stood out on deck, taking in the salty air and idyllic coastal scenery. Just as we rounded Point Scarlett, I spotted a large pod of orca in the fading light. After it grew too dark to see, I headed inside and climbed into my bunk. I was almost too excited to sleep.

I rose at dawn and immediately ran out on deck. The sky was dim and pink, and a light fog hung over the sea. We passed by the Scott Islands one by one: first the forested Lanz and Cox, then the grassy rocks of Beresford and Sartine. In the distance our destination rose from the dark blue waters—a dark green pyramid surrounded by the Pacific.

The westernmost island in the Scott Group, Triangle Island is one of the most remote islands on the Pacific coast of Canada—46 km (28.5 mi.) from the northern tip of Vancouver Island and 97 km (60 mi.) from the nearest point on the mainland of BC. As its name suggests, it is roughly triangular, about 1 km (0.6 mi.) on each side, 119 hectares (294 acres) in area, and rising just over 200 m (656 ft.) above the water at its highest point. It is a difficult place to get to. By sea it is a 125 km (77.7 mi.) voyage from Port Hardy through one of the most unpredictable stretches of water on the BC coast, with no safe anchorage at the end of the trip.

As we approached the island, Tufted Puffins, Rhinoceros Auklets, and Common Murres started to pass the boat. First in ones and two, then in dozens, and then, as the morning grew brighter, in their thousands. Triangle Island is home to the largest seabird colony in BC and we had obviously wandered into morning rush hour.

Before the Europeans arrived, indigenous people visited the island for seasonal harvests of marine mammals and seabird eggs, but there don't seem to have been any permanent settlements. A large midden on the island includes some Short-tailed Albatross, suggesting a time when the species (now one of the rarest albatrosses in the world) was fairly common in BC waters. Today, the Tlatlasikwala First Nation is considered to be the gatekeeper of all the Scott Islands, including Triangle.

Near the beginning of the twentieth century, Triangle was deemed an ideal place for a lightstation, and so in 1909–1910, a steep track was blasted in from the beach to the summit of the island, followed by the construction of a lighthouse and wireless telegraph station. Much to the embarrassment of the Department of Marine and Fisheries,

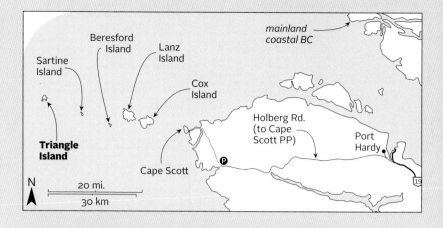

GETTING THERE

Probably the best option for those of us without a private vessel is to charter the fifty-five-foot *Naiad Explorer* through Mackay Whale Watching in Port McNeill. It comfortably fits thirty-five to forty people, has an experienced skipper, and costs about $6,000 (at time of writing) for a return trip from Port McNeill to Triangle. Split thirty ways that's fairly reasonable, and you can expect to see a number of other birds and marine wildlife along the trip. For more info, visit: whaletime.com.

however, it was soon discovered that thick fog and other poor weather conditions obscured the hilltop lighthouse from passing ships for 240 days of the year. Adding to the lighthouse-keeper's woes were the punishing winds that made it impossible to light a fire (indoors or out), shook the walls so violently that some of Triangle's inhabitants became "seasick," and as legend has it, blew their lone cow off a cliff. After several changes of disgruntled residents, the lighthouse was finally abandoned in 1919, with the wireless station crew soon to follow. Thus ended the only year-round habitation of Triangle Island.

If only those early residents had been birders! Triangle Island is now most famous for its avian residents, being home to 80,000 Rhinoceros Auklets, 60,000 Tufted Puffins, 8,000 Common Murres, and most impressive of all— 1 million Cassin's Auklets! That's roughly half the world's population of Cassin's Auklet, and the species' largest single breeding colony. Other common nesting seabirds include Fork-tailed and Leach's Storm Petrels, Pelagic Cormorants, Pigeon Guillemot, and Glaucous-winged Gulls. A few pairs of Horned Puffin are thought to breed among the Tufted each year, and a few Thick-billed Murres also appear, mixed in with the throngs of Common Murre.

At first glance, Triangle Island doesn't look like the archetypal seabird colony. To be sure, there are murres clinging to the rock cliffs on the southwestern point, and scattered gulls and puffins can be seen amid the tufted hairgrass above the cliffs. The others are underground, hidden in myriad burrows dug into the soil under the salal and salmonberry.

Triangle Island is surrounded by an important marine reserve, and the Anne Vallée Ecological Reserve (named for a seabird biologist who tragically fell to her death while working on the island) covers the land. Human visitors are strictly limited and must have permission from the provincial ministry of the Environment before setting foot on the island. Crews from the Centre for Wildlife Ecology visit the island most summers to study the seabird colonies, but for the majority of the year there are no people around.

The remoteness of Triangle Island has been a huge advantage to the birds, which can largely raise their chicks

The sun rises above Triangle Island on a calm summer morning. RUSSELL CANNINGS

away from human disturbance, but there are other dangers. Seven pairs of Peregrine Falcons regularly patrol the area, taking young birds and adults alike, and there are a growing number of Bald Eagles in the area.

BIRDING GUIDE

In addition to the access restrictions, the remoteness of Triangle Island is an obvious challenge. If you are considering a boat journey, be aware that it's around 250 km (155 mi.) for a round-trip if travelling from Port Hardy—longer from Port McNeill—and the seas can change swiftly around this part of the coast. Still, this trip is doable and I know of several birding groups that have done it.

Luckily, most of the nesting birds can be easily seen just offshore from Triangle, and there should be a good number of other species around. The weather is most stable in July–September—which is also when seabird diversity is at its height. Southern tubenose migrants like Sooty, Buller's, and Flesh-footed Shearwater will be around, along with Long-tailed, Parasitic, and Pomarine Jaegers, as well as the odd South Polar Skua. In late summer these pirates can often be seen chasing Common and Arctic Terns, as well as Sabine's Gulls and Bonaparte's Gulls.

Given the lack of birding coverage around the island for most of the year, it's remarkable how many vagrant passerines have turned up. Among the most notable are the Great Crested Flycatcher, Ash-throated Flycatcher, Northern Mockingbird, Prairie Warbler, and Chestnut-sided Warbler. If you haven't been permitted to land, don't despair. Many tired, lost birds will also land on boats, so if a small warbler or sparrow starts circling your vessel, pay attention!

2

PORT MCNEILL

A DICK AND A HOOR first brought me to Port McNeill. That's a Dickcissel and a Hooded Oriole (four-letter codes, a birder's shorthand, can be a little eye-catching sometimes!). In one of the more remarkable examples of the Patagonia Picnic Table Effect (when birders are drawn to a location to see a particular rare bird, only to find another one or more thanks to increased scrutiny of avian life in that location), these two southern species had chosen to overwinter in someone's backyard in Port McNeill.

After my first brief encounter with the area I knew I had to return. In the late summer of that same year, I spent several days camping and exploring the estuaries, beaches, and forest from the Nimpkish River to the Cluxewe, and across the strait to Malcolm Island. Everywhere I went I was struck

by the friendliness of the people, the beauty of the landscape, and how I so often had the beaches and trails to myself.

This northern part of Vancouver Island offers pristine coastal estuaries and mudflats, cloaked by ethereal coastal rainforest, and myriad productive marine habitats. It's hard to find an area more "British Columbian" in terms of scenery, culture, economy, and spirit than Port McNeill and its surrounding environs on Broughton Strait.

Some local birders and naturalists know this area well, but few outsiders (even birders from elsewhere on Vancouver Island such as Nanaimo and Victoria) know much about it. It's a little bit out of the way (but less so than Triangle) but it deserves a "must visit" reputation among birders. I hope this book will inspire a few adventurous souls to come up and explore this corner of coastal wonder.

Sointula, the lone community on Malcolm Island, was founded in 1901 by a group of Finnish settlers who rowed north from Nanaimo, seeking better living standards than the harsh conditions they'd experienced while coal mining. *Sointula* is Finnish for "place of harmony," and this name still rings true today, whether you're exchanging idle chat with the locals in BC's oldest co-op store or watching a pod of orcas pass close to the beach as eagles and gulls circle high overhead. This is also one of the better places in BC to scope

◄ The Barred Owl has been a British Columbian resident for less than seventy years (spreading from the east), but it has found the Pacific west coast very much to its liking. They are now common throughout most forest habitats on Vancouver Island, particularly where old cedar and hemlock snags provide nesting opportunities. ILYA POVALYAEV

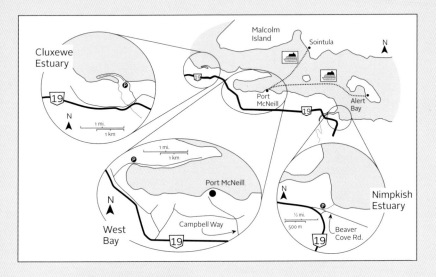

GETTING THERE

Port McNeill town centre and ferry terminal are well signed off Hwy. 19. It takes 2.5 hours to drive here from Campbell River, and just over 30 minutes from Port Hardy. Port Hardy is the closest commercial airport with flights from Vancouver, Victoria, and Nanaimo.

Fork-tailed Storm Petrels from land. Leach's Storm Petrels are scarcer but still possible to spot. Look for them during the ferry crossing or on any of the prominent headlands on the island (e.g., Bere Point).

As with any area, the birding will vary depending on the time of year. August–October is probably the best time to visit the Port McNeill area as the weather is most settled then and it's the peak of shorebird and passerine migration, so diversity is relatively high. Winters up here are wet and chilly, but west coast residents like Anna's

Hummingbird (near town only), Steller's Jay, Pacific Wren, and Spotted Towhee will still be present, as will wintering Golden-crowned and "Sooty" Fox Sparrows. Water bird diversity is also high in Broughton Strait in winter, with good numbers of sea-ducks, loons, grebes, cormorants, and alcids (mainly Common Murre, Pigeon Guillemot, Rhinoceros Auklet, and Marbled Murrelet). Spring is, of course, a very exciting time for birding anywhere. It is usually wetter than fall, but the return of southern migrants, as well as the passing exodus of seabirds and the enticing chance of vagrants, make for very enjoyable birding. Although water bird numbers are lowest during the summer nesting season, it's a great time to explore the back country for displaying Sooty and Ruffed Grouse, as well as territorial songsters like Pacific-slope Flycatcher, Hammond's Flycatcher, Hermit Thrush, Swainson's Thrush, Black-throated Gray Warbler, Townsend's Warbler, and Western Tanager.

BIRDING GUIDE

If you're intending to scope the local shorebird flocks in winter, spring, or late summer/fall, it is very important to check the tide times beforehand (easily done online). Each site is a little different, but in general it's best to arrive around midtide as it's heading for high. This allows you to set up and let the birds come to you. Arriving on a falling tide can also be fine as long as the birds are close enough. In most places, high tide covers all the foraging habitat and the birds leave for offshore roost sites inaccessible by birders. At low tide, the birds are very spread out and you'll have to squelch your way across wet mudflats to get good views.

If you plan on taking your car on the ferry to Sointula and/or Alert Bay, contact BC Ferries beforehand to inquire about arrival times. These smaller ferries can fill up quickly.

Below are some of my favourite sites in the area, ordered from southeast to northwest. Local birders have also come up with a brochure for the area which should be available in Port McNeill and Sointula.

NIMPKISH ESTUARY Beginning at the southeast edge of the area (presumably where most visitors will be coming from), this is the first stop of interest for birders.

From the Sayward turnoff on Hwy. 19, drive north for 121 km (75 mi.) then turn right onto Beaver Cove Rd. (if you cross the Nimpkish River you've gone too far), and make an immediate left onto a gravel track. On the right side of this old road, you'll see a track leading through the woods to the beach. It's possible to drive all the way to the estuary but the track is often fraught with deep muddy ruts and overgrown alders. It's only a 300 m (328 yd.) walk, so I recommend leaving your car along this gravel side road (ensure that other vehicles can get past, of course) and walking.

From Port McNeill, head south on Hwy. 19; 1.7 km (1 mi.) beyond the Nimpkish River Bridge, turn left on Beaver Cove Rd., and make an immediate left onto the gravel track.

The mudflats south of the river mouth provide some of the best shorebird habitat in the region, with thousands of Western Sandpipers passing through in April–May and August–October, joined by lesser numbers of Black-bellied Plover, Semipalmated Plover, Least Sandpiper, Semipalmated Sandpiper, Sanderling, Black Turnstone, Ruddy Turnstone, Surfbird, and Short-billed Dowitcher.

In spring and fall, the coastal waters around Port McNeill and Johnstone Strait can be fantastic for watching water bird migration. Here a group of American Wigeon pass Malcolm Island on their southward fall passage with the Coast Mountains of the mainland in the background. GORDON CURRY

From late fall to early spring, expect flocks of Dunlin; Killdeer are present off and on throughout the year. Rarer species that are still expected annually include Pacific Golden-Plover, Marbled Godwit, and Red Knot. The usual mix of migratory dabbling ducks are also common during the spring/fall passage as well as in winter, and more than ten species of gulls, including Thayer's Gull (outside the summer months) are annual visitors here.

WEST BAY In an area that's already under-birded, this site is probably one of the least known and visited, despite being one of the better shorebirding sites in the area. I don't actually know what this bay is called because it doesn't appear on any maps, so I've taken the liberty of naming it myself.

The forestry roads to get here should be drivable for all vehicles, but watch out for logging trucks and drive carefully when the road is wet. From the junction of Campbell Way and Hwy. 19 (the main turnoff to Port McNeill), head west toward Port Hardy for 3.7 km (2.3 mi.) then turn right at a crossroads onto a well-maintained gravel road. Stay left at the first junction, 350 m/yd. along; after an additional 950 m/yd., turn left again. You'll get onto a relatively straight stretch that parallels the highway and some powerlines; after 2.4 km (1.5 mi.), turn right. This track will curve back to the northeast. Drive for 1.3 km (0.8 mi.). Stay right at a minor junction to keep to the main road until you reach an obvious wider section where you can turn around and park. A short trail leads down to the north side of West Bay.

Expect a similar mix of species to that in the Nimpkish Estuary. For the best experience here, be prepared to walk across the mudflats to view all corners of the bay. Bring rubber boots if you don't want your toes to get wet. Although it's possible to scope most of the bay without setting foot on the mud, many of the birds will be far away and, if the tide is low, many more will be out of view around the corner to the east.

CLUXEWE ESTUARY Just over 9 km (5.6 mi.) from the Port McNeill turnoff (heading northwest toward Port Hardy), watch for Cluxewe Resort signs on the right. Park near the Cluxewe Resort office, let them know what you're up to, and then start your birding by scanning the grassland/wetland habitat of the estuary directly to the west. This area can be quiet at times, but Short-eared Owl and Mountain Bluebird are possible to spot in migration, and rarer species may yet be found with more coverage.

As you move along the beach beyond the camping area, you'll get out onto the gravelly spit at the mouth of the estuary. Since there isn't much mud here, most sandpipers prefer to poke through the clumps of washed-up seaweed for invertebrates. At high tide, approach the tip of the spit carefully—it's often a roosting site for shorebirds. The gravelly spit and woody debris are also frequented by foraging flocks of American Pipit, Horned Lark, Lapland Longspur, and Snow Bunting (the latter three being uncommon but regular in fall). Finally, check through the shrubs and grassy clumps along the ridge of the spit for possible rarities among the numerous Savannah, Song, and Lincoln's Sparrows in spring/fall passage.

The Bald Eagle is one of the most recognizable birds in the world thanks to our southern neighbours, however nowhere are they more common than the coastal estuaries of British Columbia, particularly during the salmon spawning season in fall and early winter. LIRON GERTSMAN

3

SALMON RIVER
ESTUARY, SAYWARD

IF YOU COULD travel back in time to the 1970s or earlier, you could depart Port McNeill on the Inside Passage ferry and cruise down the scenic Johnstone Strait to the route's southern terminus at Port Kelsey. However, since Hwy. 19 was pushed through from Campbell River to Port Hardy in 1978, the ferry has moved north as well, giving the isolated timber village of Sayward an even quieter complexion. In the past few decades, a slowing forestry industry has affected their struggling economy and in 2006 there were only 341 residents in the Sayward Valley. Fast-forward to 2015, and visitors will see that many of the old businesses are still boarded up, but an increase in sport-fishing and eco-tourism is fostering a renewed interest in this hitherto forgotten corner of Vancouver Island.

For visiting birders, the quiet quaintness of tiny Sayward and Port Kelsey, nestled in between high coastal mountains, brooding Johnstone Strait, and the Salmon River Estuary, gives the place all the allure it needs. You'll rarely bump into another sightseer while walking the nature trails around town. As for the environment, there are few estuaries in BC that are both ecologically pristine and easily accessible to visitors.

BIRDING GUIDE

As you leave Hwy. 19 and begin the drive down the Sayward Valley, following the Salmon River, look and listen for Black-throated Gray Warblers singing from the cottonwood trees lining the river. Turn right to get onto the Salmon River Rd. (see next page) giving access to the first Nature Trust trail on the right/east side. This trail is about a 1.5 km (1 mi.) loop through mature Sitka Spruce forest and estuarine back-channel habitats, bordering on brackish marshland.

Return to your car and drive 1.1 km (0.7 mi.) northwest along the Salmon River Rd., where a second Nature Trust sign indicates the Viewing Tower Trail. The isolated lines of alders and other deciduous trees, surrounded by estuary wetlands and meadows, can act as a natural funnel for migrating songbirds. Look and listen for mixed flocks in spring and late summer. This trail is also a good way to access the estuary for scoping shorebirds. On the right tides it's possible to scope the main shorebird flocks from close to your car (see next page), but on a falling/lowish tide you can bring your scope and rubber boots out to the viewing tower, then continue on foot toward the mouth of the river.

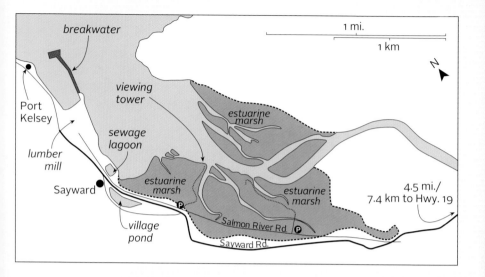

GETTING THERE

From the south, turn right/north (signed for Sayward) 60 km (37 mi.) north of Campbell River. This same junction is 129 km (80 mi.) south of Port McNeill. Access to the two short nature trails is off the Salmon River Rd. which branches off to the right from the main road to Sayward, 7.4 km (4.6 mi.) from the highway junction (after crossing the second bridge over the Salmon River). This road parallels the main road and you'll see several obvious ways to cross over to the main road near Sayward village once the estuary comes into view. There are several parallel roads that head north from Sayward through the mill and on to Port Kelsey. However, this area is quite small and once you're there it should be obvious how to navigate to each place.

Tread carefully, as this is very sensitive habitat, and be very careful not to flush foraging sandpiper and waterfowl flocks, as this is a critical staging area where birds are gaining energy to continue their migrations. Finally, be wary of hunters in duck season.

Continuing north along the Salmon River Rd., you will see Sayward village on your left. You can turn left and drive into the village just south of a small community lake (actually more of a large pond) that can hold a wide variety of dabbling and diving ducks in season. The surrounding trees are worth checking for mixed migrant flocks in migration. If you continue north instead of turning into the village, you'll see a sewage treatment pond on the right. Once again, expect a few ducks (Tufted Duck has been recorded here) as well as a decent mix of gulls, depending on the season. These ponds aren't very good for shorebirds but a birder could hypothetically run across Red-necked or Red Phalaropes spinning on the surface.

Just beyond the sewage pond, but before the sawmill, is a wide open gravel area. From here it should be obvious that walking along the estuary side of this parking area will offer a good vantage point from which to scope the mudflats of the Salmon River estuary. Tide will be a factor, of course. It's a small enough estuary that you should be able to see where the main flocks of birds are, but they won't always be close to this location; you're looking east, so afternoon is best since the sun will be behind you. Very few birders make it here, so there have yet to be any big rarity finds. However, given the good numbers of shorebirds and gulls noted on short visits here in the past, it's only a matter of time before someone strikes gold. Expect a similar species mix to that mentioned for the Port McNeill area.

At low tide, a gravel island is exposed at the mouth of the river where gulls and a few shorebirds gather. Follow the signs for a boat launch that's accessed by driving along the eastern edge of the mill and out to the end of a rocky breakwater. This spot can also be great for scoping a variety of passing seabirds farther out in Johnstone Strait, including Fork-tailed Storm Petrel and Sabine's Gull in late summer/ fall.

For Port Kelsey, head back south toward the sewage pond and turn right onto the paved road that heads north on the left/west side of the mill. This leads a short way to the main fishing docks of Kelsey Bay. You may be lucky enough to see orca whales pass close by. This was the original starting point of the BC Ferries route through the Inside Passage to Prince Rupert.

The protected waters of Comox Harbour provide limitless opportunities for viewing and photographing waterfowl outside of summer. Large flocks of Surf Scoters (pictured) and White-winged Scoters are often the most conspicuous.

LIRON GERTSMAN

4

COMOX HARBOUR

OMOX HARBOUR, FROM the tip of Goose Spit to the Courtenay River estuary and around to the Royston waterfront, is truly a lovely blend of brilliant scenery, great year-round bird variety, and ease of access for birders. Visiting birders can expect to find a variety of west-coast specialties throughout the year (both on the water and on land), while clear days afford stunning views of the Comox Glacier to the west and the waters of Georgia Strait to the east. The protected waters of the harbour team with waterfowl in winter, providing photographers with some great opportunities, particularly for White-winged Scoters at Goose Spit. Unusual sightings too are increasing with more birding coverage, including Black-tailed Gull, Slaty-backed Gull, and Canada's first and North America's second

Citrine Wagtail. The latter overwintered at a nearby farm in 2012–13. Of course, I wasn't in the country that winter.

The ease of access to all the best birding sites in this area is a tremendous asset for Comox Harbour. Public roads and paved walking/cycling trails cover nearly the entire harbour, providing easy accessibility for birders of all degrees of mobility. The relatively sheltered waters here also make the bay ideal for kayak, canoe, and sailboat exploration, allowing for closer views of many waterfowl and seabirds.

BIRDING GUIDE

With so many great options for birding this area, where you start may depend on the weather, tide-state, time of year, time of day (always best to avoid looking into the sun), and the birds you're after. If herring spawn is on, scan around for clouds of gulls to alert you to where the best birding is.

In general, all the sites mentioned are worth a visit at any time of year. If you're visiting during spring/fall shorebird migration and the tide is high, check the old rocky breakwater just off the Royston waterfront, Courtenay Airpark ponds, the small islands at the mouth of the Courtenay River, and the westerly beaches of Goose Spit (obey the access signs). By far the best place to look for shorebirds in the area is Sandy (Tree) Island at the north end of Denman Island (visible to the southeast of Goose Spit), but this requires either a private vessel or taking a ferry to Denman then walking out at low tide from the north end. At mid-/low tides, the birds can be spread out through Comox Harbour but can still be scoped well at times, especially from the walkway east of the Courtenay Airpark.

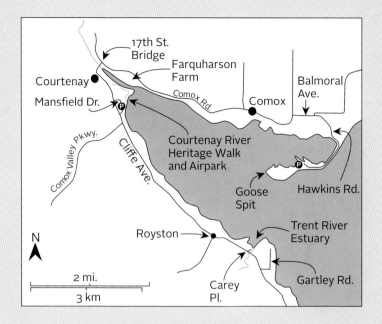

GETTING THERE

The communities of Royston, Courtenay, and Comox essentially surround the harbour and are well signed on Hwy. 19, so getting to the harbour should be fairly straightforward. To get to the Courtenay Airpark if approaching from the south on the main Island Hwy. (19), take the Comox Valley Parkway (main exit for Courtenay) all the way to Cliffe, where you'll turn left before turning onto Mansfield. Cliffe is basically the Old Island Hwy. (19A), so you can head south on Cliffe to get to Royston. Courtenay and Comox are just over an hour's drive from Nanaimo.

One relatively unknown but fantastic spot at the southeast corner of the harbour is the Trent River Estuary.

From downtown Royston, head southeast along Hwy. 19A (Old Island Hwy.); shortly after crossing the Trent River, turn left onto Gartley Rd. and follow it to the end (it turns into Gartley Point Rd.) where you can park beside a small fish hatchery. The Trent River Estuary is a wide gravel fan and right now you are on the east side of it. Walk north and northwest to get to the actual river mouth, though the birding can be great anywhere along the shoreline, particularly during herring spawn (late February to late April) when thousands of Brant, scoters, Red-breasted Mergansers, loons, grebes, and gulls gather to gobble up the beige-coloured roe. Water birds are usually around in good numbers here any time outside of early summer, although a scope is recommended for the best views. Work the grasslands and shrubby areas around here, as a Yellow Wagtail was spotted in fall 2013, and there are plenty of more common species, such as Northern Shrike (October–March), Marsh Wren, Spotted Towhee, and Purple Finch, that may be pleasing to visiting birders.

For access to the west side of the Trent River Estuary, and probably a site with better potential for interesting songbirds in migration, return to Hwy. 19A, head northwest back across the Trent River (toward Royston), and turn right at Carey Pl. You may have to park just off the highway, but at the end of this short road a trail heads down toward the estuary. This is a great spot for sparrows on migration as well as other songbirds, and of course, once you get close to the harbour, all the birds mentioned at the other Trent River site can also be encountered here.

Return to Hwy. 19A and head northwest into Royston proper. Turn right on Hayward Ave., then left on Marine Dr. Use your discretion for selecting a stop as the tide and time of year will affect conditions, but generally this is a great stretch of harbour to set up a scope. To get closest to the old breakwater (and at least fourteen shipwrecks), which is a good place for scoping shorebirds like Black-bellied Plover, turnstones, and peeps at high tide, return to Hwy. 19A and head northwest toward Courtenay for a few hundred metres/yards then turn right on Hilton Rd. A parking area here and adjacent beach and shrubs provide not only great birding but also an ideal place to scope the breakwater roost and across the waters of Comox Harbour.

Pacific Rim National Park offers birders one of the best chances in Canada to see a Wandering Tattler as they migrate to and from their northern breeding grounds. They are often accompanied by turnstones and surfbirds on barnacle-encrusted rocks. ILYA POVALYAEV

5

PACIFIC RIM
NATIONAL PARK

UNLIKE THE US coastal states of Washington, Oregon, and California, the outer coast of BC is not on the continental mainland. From the Olympic Peninsula in Washington right up to Alaska, the coast is cluttered by mazes of rock islets, large islands covered by impenetrable evergreen forests, and long fjords, stretching deep into the coastal mountains. There are therefore only a few places in BC where birders can easily access the true "West Coast"—the most popular being the area around Pacific Rim National Park on Vancouver Island.

As I write this, the rain is bucketing down outside and I'm thankful to be in a warm, dry house. I have experienced numerous moments like this in my 10+ visits to Vancouver Island's wild coast, and so it's strangely fitting that I'm actually in New Zealand. In fact, the above description of BC's coast could easily be copied and pasted into an account of New Zealand's South Island west coast. The birds would be different, of course, except for the Sooty and Buller's Shearwaters that nest in New Zealand before voyaging all the way north to spend the summer off BC's coast.

I've always felt at home in these temperate coastal forests. Although I can only vaguely recall my family's first visit to Pacific Rim National Park, I have fond memories of playing in tidal pools, exploring ethereal forests of pillowing moss, hearing the eerie song of a Varied Thrush, and rain... lots of rain. Since then, I've returned to the west coast many times. Even if the birding is slow, the scenery and atmosphere are enthralling, no matter the weather, so you always seem to leave feeling refreshed.

Most tourists will visit this area in summer, when the weather is most stable and the water is kinda, sorta warm enough to swim in. Hardy surfers play in the waves year-round, but prefer the big swells that come in the winter and spring storm seasons, though many "normal" people can also enjoy watching these huge surges from the comfort of the numerous coastal hotels and lodges in Ucluelet (most locals pronounce it "Yew-Q-lit") and around Tofino. Birding will be most interesting during migration windows (April–May and August–October), since large numbers of waterfowl, shorebirds, and songbirds pass through this area, and there is always the possibility of something rare.

BIRDING GUIDE

Note: *For most of these sites you will need to display a valid national park pass on your vehicle. These can be purchased

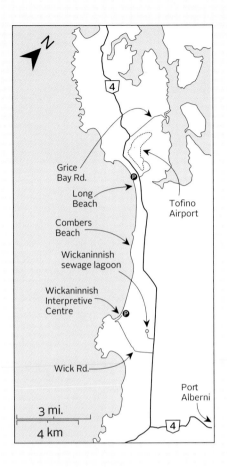

Grice
Bay Rd.

Long
Beach

Combers
Beach

Wickaninnish
sewage lagoon

Wickaninnish
Interpretive
Centre

Wick Rd.

Tofino
Airport

Port
Alberni

3 mi.

4 km

GETTING THERE

Pacific Rim National Park is on the west coast of Vancouver Island and is accessible by regular plane service from Victoria, Qualicum Beach, and Vancouver, though most visitors arrive by car or bus, using Hwy. 4. This highway is well signed off the main Island Hwy. (Hwy. 19) north of Nanaimo (follow signs for Port Alberni/Tofino). From Port Alberni it's another 90 km (56 mi.) to the junction for Ucluelet and Tofino. Turn right for Pacific Rim National Park and Tofino. The drive from Nanaimo to Pacific Rim takes around 2.5 hours, but consider breaking up your trip with stops in Parksville (pages 35–41), Cathedral Grove, or Sproat Lake.

Ethereal forests meet the wild ocean in Pacific Rim National Park. ROBIN HORN

at pay stations at Long Beach, Combers Beach, and the Kwis-itis Visitor Centre, as well as the Visitor Information Centres in Ucluelet and Tofino. There are many beach accesses and walking trails in Pacific Rim National Park, and they're all well signed off the highway as you drive toward Tofino. I would encourage visitors to explore much more than is covered below, but here are some of my favourite sites in the park itself.

KWISITIS VISITOR CENTRE (WICKANINNISH/SOUTH BEACH) From the Tofino/Ucluelet junction with Hwy. 4, proceed 4.7 km (2.9 mi.) toward Tofino then turn left onto Wick Rd., signed for the Kwisitis Visitor Centre (also spelled "Qwisitis," confusingly known as the Wickaninnish Interpretive Centre, and not to be confused with the posh Wickaninnish Inn which is closer to Tofino).

The visitor centre functions as information centre, interpretive facility, café, and gift shop (open mid-March to mid-October) and focuses on the natural and cultural heritage of Pacific Rim National Park. There is wheelchair access to the beach, where visitors can walk for miles to the north, swim in the ocean, and even go surfing if so inclined.

Look and listen around the edges of the parking area for migrating warblers in spring/fall, while the typical west-coast forest birds will be present year-round. Sanderling and other shorebirds like Western Sandpiper can be found near the water's edge in season, and flocks of gulls often loaf around near creek mouths. From here up to the north end of Long Beach is where most of Canada's Snowy Plover records come from, with the most recent one visiting in spring 2014. The barnacle-encrusted rocks between the centre and South Beach are always worth a look for rock-loving shorebirds such as Wandering Tattler and Ruddy Turnstone (April/May and August/September), Black Turnstone and Surfbird (August–May), and Rock Sandpiper (October–April). Black Oystercatchers are common year-round.

COMBERS BEACH This beach is located in between the Wickaninnish Interpretive Centre and Green Point. Look for the well-signed parking area on the left/ocean side of the highway. The sandy banks on the edge of the parking lot usually have a nesting pair of Northern Rough-winged Swallow in summer. From here, the beach is a short walk down the hill. The trail passes through a pleasant stand of west-coast rainforest and salmonberry wetland before emerging out onto the beach. The large creek that empties out here usually attracts large numbers of loafing gulls and occasionally groups of shorebirds. *Note*: *This beach is often closed in winter due to trail erosion from storm swells.

LONG BEACH/INCINERATOR ROCK 3.4 km (2.1 mi.) northwest of Green Point is the main parking lot for Long Beach (opposite the Tofino Airport road). The parking area for Incinerator Rock just down the road is essentially an extension of the same site. This is obviously another opportunity to check out the beach and seabirds offshore, but the parking lot itself is also worth a visit. Lined with alders, it is one of the best spots on the west coast for migrant passerines. Suitable habitat is relatively scarce out here along the wild coast, so the birds concentrate in these patches of broadleaf trees before continuing south (or north in spring). In late summer, large flocks of warblers can be seen in the area, and this parking lot is one of the best spots to check. Yellow-rumped Warbler, Orange-crowned Warbler, Yellow Warbler, Townsend's Warbler, Warbling Vireo, and Ruby-crowned Kinglet are some of the more common migrants encountered, but almost anything is possible in fall when many young birds stray off course. Brown Thrasher is probably one of the more notable birds encountered here over the years.

6

ENGLISHMAN RIVER ESTUARY, PARKSVILLE

According to a local legend, indigenous people in this area found the skeleton of a Caucasian man near present-day Englishman River Falls, thus giving the river its current name. Prior to that, Spanish mapmakers had named it the Rio de Grullas, presumably because of the large number of Great Blue Herons that feed around the estuary (*grulla* being Spanish for "crane").

Fast-forward to today and fortunately the dead bodies are all long-gone but there are still plenty of herons. In an area abundant with rich estuaries and beaches, the Englishman River Estuary is one of the best spots for birding year-round and it's conveniently located right beside downtown

Outside of summer, the coastline around Parksville and Qualicum teems with water birds, including the distinctive Harlequin Duck that nests in the rushing mountain rivers of the Interior before wintering in small flocks along rocky ocean shorelines of British Columbia. LIRON GERTSMAN

Parksville. A Nature Trust reserve covers 68 hectares (168 acres) of lovely coastal habitat including a tidal estuary, gravelly beach, mixed woodland, and even native grassland. A 2.4 km (1.5 mi.) loop trail, which includes a viewing tower over the estuary, on the west side of the river (Shelly Rd. access) gives visitors access to most of these habitats, while Plummer Rd. on the east side supplies another viewpoint of the estuary and easy access to the beach along Georgia Strait.

The tidal mudflats of the Englishman River Estuary are best outside of early summer when shorebird numbers are highest. Check Parksville tide times so you arrive outside of high tide, when the mud is covered. Dabbling ducks migrate through here in good numbers and many spend the winter. Mallard, American Wigeon, Northern Pintail, and Green-winged Teal are the most numerous, but a few Gadwall and Eurasian Wigeon are usually around, and sometimes the Eurasian form of the Green-winged Teal (also known as Common Teal) turns up.

Late February until the end of April is herring spawn season, so if you're lucky enough to visit when a spawn is occurring (they happen suddenly and usually only last for a couple days at any one site), you can encounter thousands of gulls—mostly Glaucous-winged, California, and Thayer's, though rarities like Glaucous and Kumlien's (Iceland) Gull are picked out annually by visitors with sharp eyes. Many other species, such as Brant, scoters, Bald Eagles, and shore-birds, take part in the herring spawn feast too. The estuary is a favoured bathing and loafing place for gulls throughout the area, so even if the herring aren't going, there's almost always a good mix of gulls outside of summer. Heermann's Gull, typically more of a Juan de Fuca/outer coast species, sometimes shows up here between August and November.

BIRDING GUIDE

There are essentially two main sections to the area known as the Englishman River Estuary: The Plummer Rd. side (east) and the Shelly Rd. side (west). Both have their advantages.

EAST SIDE For the quickest way to the tidal estuary where waders, dabbling ducks, and gulls are most likely, as well as easy access to the beach, turn north off the Old Island Hwy. (19A) on Plummer Rd. and follow it along the east side of the river. You may want to check for American Dipper along the river, especially south of the bridge. As Plummer Rd. begins to bend to the right, there is a gravel pull-off area on the left side, with a gravel track continuing straight on with a "No Thru Road" sign. This is just before Plummer Rd. leaves the forest and turns into an old subdivision.

You can park here and walk this track along the east side of the estuary. The first 350 m/yd. take you along a small side-channel of the river with lots of mixed shrubs that are great for small birds year-round. The east side of the Englishman River Estuary will be obvious. It's a small estuary, so shorebird numbers are never very high, but a good variety of species comes through regularly each spring and late summer/fall. Try to arrive outside of high tide when there is exposed mud. This trail passes a small viewing tower then ends near the north end of San Malo Crescent, where it joins up with the northwestern terminus of Mariner Way.

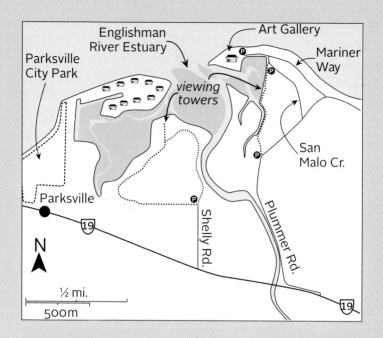

GETTING THERE

From downtown Parksville, drive east along the Old Island Hwy. Shelly Rd. is on the north side just past Tim Hortons and A&W, while Plummer Rd. is the first left after crossing the Englishman River bridge. If approaching from Nanaimo along the main highway, take Exit 46, signed for Parksville and Rathtrevor; in just over 3 km (1.9 mi.), Plummer Rd. will be on the right/north side (if you cross the bridge over the Englishman you've gone too far), and Shelly Rd. will be about 400 m/yd. past the bridge (on the right side).

Alternatively, continue along Plummer Rd., which turns into Shorewood Dr., then turn left at Mariner Way and park at the end of the road near the entrance gate for the art gallery. The eastern corner of the estuary will be obvious on the south side of the road, as will the trail described above.

You can continue on foot from this point using the directions above.

Walk south along the outside of the art gallery fence, following a little trail that winds through clumps of broom and moss. The trail then rounds the corner to the right and continues toward the mouth of the main river channel. This trail gives you more opportunity to scan the estuary. The cobblestone bars at the river mouth are where most gulls and some shorebirds concentrate, so have a scope handy if possible. As the trail fizzles out, you can clamber down some boulders onto a sandy bank and turn the corner at the end of the spit where the gallery sits. Note that this is not advisable at high tide. Everything below the tide-line is public land, so it's fine to walk around to the outer beach in front of the art gallery. From the tip of the point, it's about a 400 m/yd. walk along the beach to get to a public beach access through-way which will lead you back onto Mariner Way just a few metres from your car, or the end of that estuary trail mentioned earlier. Along the beach, scan for all the water birds and keep an eye on the mowed lawn around the art gallery, as uncommon open-country birds like Mountain Bluebird and Western Meadowlark turn up here in migration and mixed flocks of geese are regular in fall, winter, and spring.

WEST SIDE For access to the west side of the estuary, and its 2.4 km (1.5 mi.) loop trail plus viewing-tower, park at the north end of Shelly Rd., which turns off the Old Island Hwy. (19A) just west of the bridge over the Englishman River. From the parking lot, head due west along the trail that separates the forest from some houses. About 300 m/ yd. from the parking lot, the trail bends to the right and the habitat will open up to the west. This is the Shelly Creek estuary, a very important part of the Englishman conservation area as a whole. You can leave the path and explore this expansive meadow area, but tread carefully and do not take dogs with you, as the tidal creek is an important feeding area for shorebirds like Wilson's Snipe, Greater Yellowlegs, and Long-billed Dowitcher, as well as Green-winged Teal and other dabbling ducks. In late fall, you have a chance of flushing Lapland Longspur from these weedy meadows, so make sure you familiarize yourself with their dry rattle.

The main trail that follows the western edge of the forest gets to its northern-most point at an obvious viewing tower. You'll have a different angle on the river mouth than that offered by the Plummer Rd. side. Scan carefully for ducks, shorebirds, and gulls with your scope as some birds can blend in well with the large cobbles along the river.

Continue clockwise along the trail as it sweeps back south through the forest to the Shelly Rd. parking area. Most of the westcoast specialty forest birds like Hutton's Vireo, Chestnut-backed Chickadee, Bewick's Wren, Pacific Wren, and Varied Thrush can be spotted here, and both Barred and Great Horned Owl are sometimes spotted roosting close to the trail.

Thanks to Victoria's relatively mild winters, Anna's Hummingbirds are now more abundant here than anywhere else in their range. Listen for the male's scratchy song as he perches atop a prominent twig. LIRON GERTSMAN

7

VICTORIA WATERFRONT

OES ANY CANADIAN city offer a more impressive selection of top-notch, year-round birding sites within a small urban area than Victoria? While BC's capital and its suburbs have seen massive expansion in the past few decades, many places within the city limits of Victoria and Saanich still offer local and visiting birders a diverse array of species throughout the year, a wonderful cross-section of Pacific coast specialties, and the opportunity to discover mind-blowing rarities. Victoria, one of the mildest winter cities in Canada, holds the world record for Anna's Hummingbirds on a Christmas Bird Count (over 1,000!).

Since Victoria is located near the southern tip of Vancouver Island, the area is a natural funnel for birds travelling along the Pacific flyway, and many concentrate at these last points of land before flying across the Juan de Fuca Strait to the Olympic Peninsula in Washington. This makes fall birding very exciting, but spring can be equally productive, especially after a good morning shower.

There are so many great places to bird in Victoria it can be difficult to decide where to start. I figure the best place to start is right in downtown. Within just over 1 km (0.6 mi.) of Victoria Harbour, there are two easily accessible sites offering a lovely cross-section of Victoria birding, including diverse parkland, rocky shoreline, and the wonderful seabird-watching opportunities of the Juan de Fuca Strait. The Victoria Natural History Society's website (vicnhs.bc.ca) is also worth checking out.

BIRDING GUIDE

These sites are close together and close to downtown Victoria with ample footpaths and bus stops, so you have a choice between driving, cycling, or walking. For Clover Point, a scope is highly recommended as there's usually a good mix of water birds feeding and flying by just a bit out of binocular range.

BEACON HILL PARK This is essentially Victoria's version of Central Park. With over 135 hectares (330 acres) of mixed woodland and grassland, there are plenty of corners to explore. In spring and fall, this is a great place to observe songbird migration, with good numbers of vireos, flycatchers, thrushes, warblers, and sparrows passing through. In late fall and early winter, look for lost vagrants that get mixed in with the resident flocks of Chestnut-backed

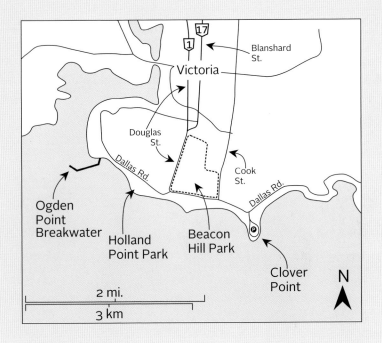

GETTING THERE

There are a number of ways to visit Victoria, including regular flights from Vancouver, two ferries from Washington State, and a BC Ferries service from Tsawwassen (Vancouver) to Swartz Bay at the north end of the Saanich Peninsula (roughly 1 hour's drive to downtown Victoria). If driving from Nanaimo, it takes around 1.5 hours to get to Victoria along Hwy. 1. Whether travelling from the Nanaimo direction or Swartz Bay, follow the signs for downtown Victoria. Just beyond the provincial Legislature and Royal BC Museum, Douglas and Blanchard Streets merge; continue south along the west side of Beacon Hill Park until you hit Dallas Rd. at a T-junction.

Ever-present gull flocks dot the rocks and mowed grass of Clover Point.

Chickadees (the only chickadee on Vancouver Island), Bush-tits, and Golden-crowned Kinglets. Some recent standouts include Blackburnian Warbler and Blue-gray Gnatcatcher. A few feral Indian Peafowl reside in the park, with birders continually arguing over their "countability." There is also a standard city duck pond in Beacon Hill—Goodacre Lake. Mallards dominate, but a few other species join the mix during the winter months, including the occasional Eurasian Wigeon. This is a wonderful place to bird year-round.

CLOVER POINT Consisting only of a parking lot, an open grassy area, and a rocky shoreline, there isn't much to Clover Point, but for some reason the birds seem to like it. This is likely due to its location as the southernmost point along this stretch of coast. Even with the steady stream of humans passing through the area, the birds continue to show themselves, much to the delight of local and visiting birders. To reach it, head east for a few hundred metres/yards on Dallas Rd. from the south/ocean end of Beacon Hill Park, then turn right into the obvious ring-shaped parking lot at Clover Point.

With at least sixteen larid species recorded, gulls are without question the signature bird group to watch for here. Winter seems to be the best time for diversity, but each season brings a different mix. Throughout the year, the most abundant species is Glaucous-winged along with a good number of "mutts," also known as "Olympic Gulls" or "Puget Sound Gulls." These hybrids are mostly crosses between Glaucous-winged and Western Gulls, but sometimes it's hard to tell! Pure Western Gulls are sometimes present in small numbers in the winter and to a lesser extent in the fall and spring, but they can be tricky to separate from the "Western-like" hybrids. To count an adult bird as pure Western, experts generally look for six things: Pure white head, greenish eyes, bright yellow orbital ring, dark mantle, jet-black primaries, and large orange-yellow bill. Heermann's Gulls become common in late July/early August and remain in the area into November before heading back south; California Gulls can be seen through most of the year but especially during spring and fall migration periods; Herring Gulls are less common but are still regularly seen outside of early summer; Ring-billed Gulls are surprisingly rare in the Victoria region but show up occasionally outside of the nesting season; Mew Gulls are common outside of summer; Glaucous Gulls are rare but regular in winter (though beware of pale/bleached Glaucous-winged Gulls); Thayer's Gulls are common from late fall to early winter; and Kumlien's (Iceland) Gulls are rare—around one individual is reported each winter. Bonaparte's Gulls pass through in good numbers during spring and fall and are occasionally spotted in winter. The rest of the species list consists of big-time rarities, including Red-legged Kittiwake, Ross's Gull, and Black-tailed Gull.

It's not ALL about the gulls though; some days you may see very few. As a prominent point of land, Clover Point is a great place to set up a scope and scan the nearby bays and off-shore waters. Common species outside of summer include Surf and White-winged Scoter, Harlequin Duck, Common Loon, Pacific Loon, Red-throated Loon, Western Grebe, Red-necked Grebe, Horned Grebe, Common and Red-breasted Mergansers, all three cormorant species, as well as alcids like Common Murre, Pigeon Guillemot, Rhinoceros Auklet, and Marbled Murrelet. Between late November and early March you might even be lucky enough to see small groups of Ancient Murrelets shuttling back and forth up the Juan de Fuca Strait.

In addition, open-country passerines like American Pipit (spring/fall), Snow Bunting (fall/winter), and Lapland Long-spurs (fall) are found annually in the grassy fringes around the parking area. Shorebirds are often seen around the barnacle-encrusted boulders; Rock Sandpiper is possible in winter.

8

IONA ISLAND, RICHMOND

MANY LOCATIONS ARE as stunningly beautiful as they are great for birding. Iona Island is not one of them. To be fair, it has its moments, though: The late summer sun setting over the ocean while staging flocks of swallows mass over the cattail ponds, or clear and crisp spring mornings when the brambles are filled with warbler song as chattering Marsh Wrens dart through bulrushes and Purple Martins chirp high overhead, celebrating the end of a long northward journey, are indisputable examples of utter beauty.

But let's be honest. The main attraction for birders is that Iona hosts Vancouver's largest sewage-processing plant, pumping 500 million litres (132 million gallons) of primary sewage into the Strait of Georgia every day.

Everyone knows that sewage ponds are great for ducks so you can expect to see a great variety of waterfowl at Iona, especially outside of summer. Here a rare Tufted Duck stands beside three other species—can you name them?

The sad thing is, I know some of you read that last passage and got sincerely excited. Sewage lagoons are, after all, some of the most cherished birding locations across the world. For instance, it has been claimed that the most visited birding site in Australia—a country known for its colourful parrots and spectacular natural scenery—is in fact the Werribee Sewage Farm just outside of Melbourne. However, a sunny day at Iona does provide some pleasant views of distant mountains as well as Vancouver Island and the smaller Gulf and San Juan Islands. With close to fifty shorebird species recorded at Iona and just under three hundred species overall, Iona Island has undeniably been one of BC's most productive birding sites since the 1960s. Among the thousands of shorebirds and waterfowl that pass through each year have been some fantastic rarities such as North America's first Spoon-billed Sandpiper in 1978—allegedly photographed by someone who launched a rowboat into the sewage lagoons (birders are dedicated!). Other standouts include Garganey, Curlew Sandpiper, multiple records of Little and Red-necked Stints, BC's only record of Common Moorhen, and Northern Wheatear.

Whether you count yourself a sewage fan or not, there really is something for everyone on Iona Island. In addition to the traditional treatment plant cells (this fenced-off area known as the "Inner Ponds" requires a password to gain entrance; see Birding Guide), there are public trails around the more natural-looking "Outer Ponds," and on most days during migration season, the Iona Bird Observatory runs a banding station. A series of mist-nets is set up in the bramble patches and cottonwood forest on the north side of the fenced-off sewage lagoons. Birds fly into the nets, then trained volunteers extract them, identify them, weigh them, measure them, attach a small aluminum band to their leg, and send them on their way. By retrapping birds here and elsewhere, we can get a sense of how long these birds live, where they migrate to, and what kinds of numbers are passing through a given area. (See ionaislandbirdobservatory. blogspot.com.)

Those angling to put more distance between themselves and the wafting lagoons could try Iona Beach on the northwest side of the public toilets. This can actually be a rather lovely place to stroll on a sunny day, though the bay is too shallow to make swimming worthwhile.

Finally, there's the Iona South Jetty, which is essentially a service road for the 4 km (2.5 mi.) long pipe that shoots the treated water out into the sea. It's a great place to scope water birds from close to the end, and there are usually a few interesting things to be found along the rocky breakwater itself. (See below.)

BIRDING GUIDE

Your approach to Iona Island will take you along the perimeter of the Vancouver International Airport. When the road turns north, you cross a causeway to Iona Island; the South Jetty will be visible on your left and MacDonald Slough with its bundles of timber will be on the right. The road swings left at the entrance to the sewage facility. Continue left through the gate (generally open from 7 am until just after dusk), then drive 200 m/yd. to park on the right by a small gate and a wooden kiosk. This is the main entrance to the Inner Ponds. You'll need a four-digit code to pass through

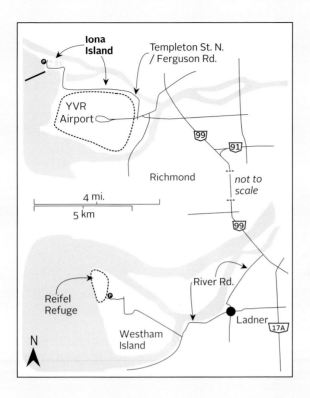

Iona Island

Templeton St. N. / Ferguson Rd.

YVR Airport

99

91

Richmond

not to scale

4 mi.

5 km

River Rd.

Reifel Refuge

99

Ladner

17A

Westham Island

N

GETTING THERE

Follow the signs to the main international airport off Hwy. 99. Once on Sea Island (where the airport is), turn right/north onto Templeton St. N.; this will become Grauer Rd., then Ferguson Rd. as you skirt the northern boundary of the airport. After a series of speed-bumps the road turns north and crosses the Iona Island Causeway. Immediately after passing through a yellow road gate, pull over on the right side of the road near the gate in the fence. This is the entrance to the Inner Ponds. For the main parking area, proceed another couple hundred metres/yards to a building with public toilets opposite cattail-fringed wetlands (known as the Outer Ponds). Although it's close to the airport, at time of writing no buses run to Iona, and it's a long walk from the main terminal for birders looking for something to do during a layover. It's probably most practical to take a taxi and then arrange a pick-up time for your return to the airport.

here (send a message to the folks at naturevancouver.ca prior to your visit). If you lift the wooden flap of the kiosk you'll find a notebook for recording recent sightings at the lagoons, though in recent years it hasn't been kept very up to date. Birders are generally permitted in here but you must first register yourself as a visitor through Nature Vancouver. Another gate, on the west side of the lagoons, closer to the banding station, requires the same password. Before or after heading into the Inner Ponds, pop across the road to where a fence surrounds a small outflow pond. This can be good for spotting waterfowl outside of summer and some shorebirds in season (including Solitary Sandpiper—a scarce species on the BC coast—in August).

As in most sewage lagoons, the water levels in each cell vary throughout the year. If conditions are right during spring and fall, the ponds can literally fill up with "peeps." Western Sandpipers are usually most numerous in April and August/September while Dunlin take over in late fall and during winter. Other regular species (in season) include Semipalmated Plover, Greater and Lesser Yellowlegs, Spotted Sandpiper, Least Sandpiper, Pectoral Sandpiper, and Long-billed Dowitcher. Unfortunately, overall numbers have greatly decreased at this location in recent years, partly due to different sewage treatment practices and the constantly changing ecology of the Fraser Delta, but also due to significant population declines in many species. Still, these ponds are always worth a check as they continue to turn up great birds, both in the ponds and in the brushy patches around them. Shorebird numbers and diversity are highest in August/September, and a visit at high tide (when birds get pushed off the foreshore) will give you the best chance of seeing a lot of birds. Outside of summer, the Inner Ponds should also be filled with a good mix of waterfowl. Dabbling ducks like wigeon, pintail, and teal predominate, but good numbers of diving ducks can be seen as well, including Tufted Duck every couple years (October–March).

After checking the inner sewage ponds, continue along the road and park in the main lot near the washrooms. From here you can bird the foreshore and trails through the brambles that lead around the Outer Ponds. Many of the typical marsh species nest around these larger ponds, like Pied-billed Grebe, American Bittern, Virginia Rail, Sora, Marsh Wren, Common Yellowthroat, and Red-winged Blackbird. This is also one of the few local breeding locations of Yellow-headed Blackbird. The trails behind the marshes that lead into the cottonwoods are particularly productive during migration season, and you may run into the biologists who run the local banding station. Sparrows are abundant throughout much of the year, and especially outside the breeding season when hordes of Fox and Golden-crowned Sparrows head south to join the resident flocks of White-crowned Sparrows, Song Sparrows, and Spotted Towhees.

Iona Beach and the adjacent foreshore can be a good place for shorebirds and gulls, especially on a rising tide. Walking through the mixed grassland and shrubs that border the area, particularly north of the parking lot (along a spit known as the North Jetty), can be very worthwhile during spring and fall, as you never know what you might kick up among the regular pipits, sparrows, and meadowlarks. Short-eared Owls are regular here around dusk during the fall months, and Purple Martins nest in the boxes set up on the old pilings along the Fraser River just northeast of the main parking lot.

Alternatively, walk out along the Iona South Jetty. This 4 km (2.5 mi.) long jetty is accessible by foot or bicycle only, and local birders like it for several reasons. First, it's one of the most reliable spots in the Vancouver area to see Horned Lark (fall), Snow Bunting (fall/winter), and Lapland Long-spur (fall) which forage on the ground along the edges of the jetty, typically out toward the tip. In the winter of 2004/05, a McKay's Bunting was seen by many, hanging out with Snow Buntings. Second, the South Jetty can be a good place to look for rock-loving shorebirds (like turnstones and surfbirds) in the right season, particularly the locally rare Wandering Tattler (May and August). Flocks of Sanderling, Western Sandpipers, and Dunlin often roost along the rocks near the tip during high tide. Large flocks of gulls (and the occasional jaeger in late summer and fall) sometimes congregate near the tip, where a long pipe pumps out treated sewage water. Since the jetty juts into Georgia Strait, birders have a way to get closer to the rafts of scoters, mergansers, loons, grebes, alcids, etc., that are only dots when viewed from the mainland.

9

REIFEL REFUGE, DELTA

WITH OVER 250 species recorded, the George C. Reifel Migratory Bird Sanctuary—Reifel Refuge for short —is unquestionably one of BC's top birding spots. It's no secret either, with thousands of visitors annually, including families looking to feed some ducks, school groups, professional photographers, beginner birders, hardcore twitchers, biologists, and people who just want an interesting day out. I'm making it sound like a place jampacked with humans, but most days at Reifel are quite peaceful with plenty of quiet corners where birders and photographers can enjoy close views of a variety of birds. If you visit on a weekday morning you might even have the entire place to yourself.

Visitors to Reifel will notice that many of the birds have grown accustomed to humans. This includes perhaps the tamest wild Sandhill Cranes in North America—warning—they do peck! ILYA POVALYAEV

Because it's a private sanctuary, there are some key differences between Reifel and other migratory bird sanctuaries. First of all, there's a fee as well as limited visiting hours. You'll also notice right away how tame many of the ducks and other birds are. This is because there are bird-feeding stations throughout the sanctuary for blackbirds, sparrows, finches, towhees, hummingbirds, and chickadees, and you can purchase bags of seed at the entrance office to feed the ducks. The resident birds, including a family of Sandhill Cranes, are also quite used to humans now, so will practically let you pet them. Some may think this gives the place a bit of a zoo-like atmosphere, but there are many species that are truly wild and rely on this expansive area of freshwater wetlands, shrubs, reed-beds, and tidal marsh for nesting, wintering, and migratory staging habitat. The ease of viewing makes this a brilliant place for new birders to work on their identification skills, and photographers love it for the great shooting opportunities.

Below is a detailed account of the different sections of Reifel and what you might encounter at different times of the year. The property is accessible every day of the year from 9 am to 5 pm. Entry is $5 for adults ($3 for children/seniors) with annual and life memberships available. Free guided walks are usually offered on Sunday mornings. (Call the refuge at 604-946-6980 or visit www.reifelbirdsanctuary.com for more info.)

BIRDING GUIDE

During shorebird migration (primarily April–May and July–November), try to visit close to high tide as this is when birds will be pushed into the outer ponds of Reifel from the tidal banks along the Fraser Delta. Ideally, arrive a little before high tide, walk out to the West Field, and wait for the shorebird flocks to come in for close views. No matter the tide state, however, Reifel is a fabulous place to visit on any day of the year, as there will always be plenty to look at. With around 5 km (3 mi.) of trails (all accessible for wheelchairs and strollers/prams), there's plenty of choice.

After the entrance gate, the road continues another 600 m/yd. to the parking area and gift shop. The shallow channel along the entrance road is worth scanning for ducks other than the abundant Mallards, and the cedar trees on the left occasionally host roosting owls. At any time of year, it's worth walking along this road to look and listen for songbirds.

Although the best birding is generally beyond the entrance gate, it's often quite productive to wait around in the parking area to see what's flying around. Scan the skies for swallows and raptors, and check through the mass of Mallards for other species such as Wood Duck and American Wigeon. While paying your fees, ask the staff about recent sightings. There is a weekly list posted, as well as a logbook for daily sightings, which will give you a good idea of what birds to look out for as you make your way around the trails. The staff can also advise you what routes have been most productive lately.

After passing through the pay station you may want to look at the pond directly behind the warming hut. For most of the year the water is high, so it's mostly waterfowl that will be here, but sometimes in late summer there is exposed mud which can attract both Yellowlegs species, Long-billed

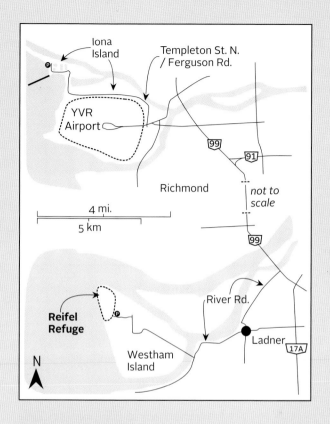

GETTING THERE

From the north along Hwy. 99 through Richmond, take the River Rd. exit immediately after passing through the tunnel. When you get to a T-junction, turn left/east on Elliott St.; in 400 m/yd. turn right at the major intersection in downtown Ladner. This will turn into River Rd. again. Watch for signs for Westham Island and Reifel Refuge on the right. From the east on Hwy. 99, take the Hwy. 17A exit, turn right onto Ladner Trunk Rd. (toward Ladner village centre), and follow the main road until it turns into River Rd. The one-lane bridge over Canoe Pass (an arm of the Fraser separating Westham Island from the mainland) is a reliable place to see "countable" Mute Swans. (The ones at Stanley Park near downtown Vancouver have clipped wings and are therefore not considered wild.) Drive 3.8 km (2.4 mi.) from the bridge and turn left down the Reifel entrance road.

Looking north across the flooded "West Field" from the viewing tower at Reifel Refuge. ILYA POVALYAEV

Dowitcher, and a few other wader species. On the other side of the path, just a bit farther up, is a large hawthorn covering a small slough. This is the traditional roosting area for several Black-crowned Night-Herons that are annual at Reifel outside of summer. If they aren't here, continue to the large oxbow on the right. Check the thick vegetation on either side for the pale forms of sleeping night-herons.

Not far from the main visitor centre, you'll reach a major trail junction with a trail map. The long straight trail to the right follows a line of tall firs to the northeast corner of the refuge. Fox Sparrows (outside of summer), Song Sparrows, Spotted Towhees, and Black-capped Chickadees are abundant along this trail; look and listen overhead for flocks of Golden-crowned Kinglets and Brown Creeper. Northern Saw-whet Owls can sometimes be found roosting in the thick clumps of fir and holly, but be sure not to get too close or use flash-photography. Anyone caught disturbing owls will be asked to leave the reserve immediately.

Starting back from that main junction, you can also choose from any of the interior trails that meander through ponds, oxbows, shrubby areas, and wetlands. Expect close views of waterfowl, with the best diversity occurring in winter. These trails are also great in spring and fall for migrating warblers and other songbirds, with several rarities being spotted over the years, including Prothonotary Warbler and Green-tailed Towhee.

A tall blue viewing tower in the northwestern section of the refuge provides great views of the northern Fraser Delta as well as Vancouver Island to the west (on a clear day). It's a great place to scope most of the West Field, the series of large ponds that stretch south from the tower. A good mix of waterfowl is usually present year-round with all three teal species possible during May–September. In spring and fall migration, and for much of the winter, the tower is also a great spot for watching thousands of Snow Geese transit from feeding grounds along the river delta and mudflats to the farm fields of Westham Island and Richmond. If they're feeding in the fields of Westham Island, they'll be hard to miss as you drive to or from Reifel. Scan through these flocks for the uncommon Blue Goose (a dark morph of the Snow) and even rarer species like Emperor and Ross's Goose.

These shallow ponds along the west dyke are also the best places to find mixed flocks of shorebirds, especially around high tide when they're pushed off the muddy banks of the Fraser Delta. During the peak migration windows (April and August–September), expect good numbers of Western Sandpipers with lesser numbers of Least and Semi-palmated Sandpipers. Both Lesser and Greater Yellowlegs are common in season, with Greaters sometimes sticking around into winter. Long-billed Dowitcher is a common visitor to these ponds in spring and fall, with large numbers of juveniles passing through in September/October, sometimes massing in the thousands. In general, Short-billed Dowitchers are uncommon to rare at Reifel in the spring and fall passage, though there is a window in late July/early August when they can outnumber Long-billed in the West Field. Short-bills tend to prefer the tidal mudflats while Long-bills favour freshwater feeding areas. Some Long-bills linger into winter and even remain until spring, so if you ever see a dowitcher in BC after November, it's practically guaranteed to be a Long-billed. Dunlin are also common in season (mainly October–April), and both Wilson's and Red-necked Phalaropes make brief appearances each spring and late summer. Pectoral Sandpipers are regular, mainly in fall; check closely for Stilt Sandpiper in August–September and Sharp-tailed Sandpiper in September–October as they're both annual here. September is probably the best month for shorebird diversity; overall, Reifel has racked up over forty species, including some mouth-watering rarities like Spotted Redshank (three!), Wood Sandpiper, Ruff, and Temminck's Stint!

10

BOUNDARY BAY, DELTA

OASTING SOME OF the highest concentrations of migratory waterfowl and shorebirds in western North America, Boundary Bay is truly one of BC's birding gems. A significant portion of North America's Northern Pintail, American Wigeon, and Dunlin populations rely on the rich mudflats of the bay for wintering grounds, and many other species use the intertidal habitats and adjacent fields and shrubs throughout the year. At over 60 km (37 mi.) across, it's too big to cover in its entirety here, so I've selected a 6.8 km stretch of the raised walking/cycling dyke trail that I think best represents the potential of the area. Over 250 species of bird have been recorded, including close to 50 species of shorebirds, in this area.

Boundary Bay is one of the most important pit-stops for migrating shorebirds on the Pacific Flyway, and so it makes a wonderful place to practice your shorebird identification skills. Here a Dunlin (right) rests next to its smaller cousin, the Western Sandpiper. ILYA POVALYAEV

While migration season is obviously an exciting time for shorebirds and other migrants, the winter months can be equally productive, with some of the highest concentrations of raptors in North America, attracted by the abundance of waterfowl, Dunlin, and Black-bellied Plovers out on the bay and good populations of small rodents that live in the weedy fields and meadows. When the tide is in, scope farther offshore to see loons, grebes, and diving ducks.

The Boundary Bay dyke trail, open to the public for walking and cycling throughout the year, begins in the Beach Grove neighbourhood of Tsawwassen in the west and ends at Mud Bay Park in South Surrey. This chapter covers the area from the foot of 72nd St., east to the foot of 104th St. This land is relatively flat and offers wonderful views of the North Shore Mountains to the north and Mount Baker (in Washington State) to the southeast. As you drive along each access road, scan prominent trees, powerlines, and cell towers for ever-watchful raptors. Fallow fields can attract large numbers of loafing gulls, as Metro Vancouver's main landfill is not far away. These fields can also be good for roosting shorebirds at high tide.

In the winters of 2011/12 and 2012/13, birders were treated to a major influx of Snowy Owls to the region. At their height, there were as many as forty of these enthralling Arctic owls viewable in one place, creating excitement not only for the birding community, but for the public as a whole.

Snowy Owls are open-country birds, adapted to the Arctic tundra. Therefore, when they turn up at places like Boundary Bay, they tend to roost in obvious, unprotected situations like the top of a stump or log. This leaves them exposed to disturbance from humans trying to get a closer look or a photograph. Furthermore, they're often exhausted and starving by the time they reach southern Canada or the northern half of the USA. Normally they would stay up north, but every five years or so, lemming and other rodent populations can crash in a certain area of the Arctic, forcing some owls (especially younger birds) to head south to seek out other food sources.

During those two winters, literally hundreds of people turned up each day to see them. Most observers kept a respectful distance but many got too close, and it wasn't uncommon to see one owl surrounded by six or more people with cameras. As the people inched closer, the bird would spook and fly away. In some cases, photographers were seen flushing the birds on purpose to get a flight shot. Not only were birds being harassed, but these incidents instigated a number of confrontations that pitted photographers against birders. This frustrated me greatly, as no matter where one lies on the birder-photographer spectrum, at no point should we lose sight of the fact that our common interest is the birds. It stands to reason that each individual bears a responsibility to enjoy their pastime in a way that is both environmentally ethical and sustainable.

BIRDING GUIDE

A spotting scope is highly recommended for all sites in this chapter.

72ND ST. Beginning from the west side of our selected section of Boundary Bay, 72nd St. is well signed off the

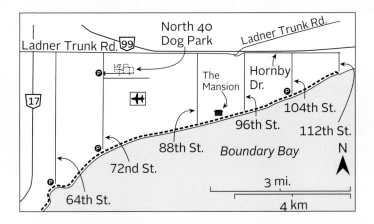

72nd St. is reached by turning south off Ladner Trunk Rd. (Hwy. 10), 2.4 km (1.5 mi.) east of the Ladner Trunk/Hwy. 17A junction just east of downtown Ladner. If travelling south on Hwy. 99 from Vancouver and Richmond, take Exit 28 for Hwy. 17A then turn left at the first major intersection on Ladner Trunk Rd. For those approaching from Hwy. 99 south (e.g., from White Rock), take Exit 20 onto Ladner Trunk Rd. (westbound) by crossing back over the freeway. From there, it's 4.6 km (2.9 mi.) west to 72nd St. For 104th, turn onto Hornby Dr. off Ladner Trunk Rd. and continue east until you see 104th on the right. The site is at the same Exit 20 (south side of Hwy. 99) junction mentioned above.

Ladner Trunk Rd. (Hwy. 10) at a set of lights (you'll be turning south). When approaching from Ladner Trunk during migration periods, scan the large turf farm on the west side of 72nd St. Killdeer will dominate, but occasionally Buff-breasted Sandpipers are recorded in August/September, and a good mix of gulls can be found here in winter.

From the south end of 64th St. (another access point to the dyke closer to Ladner) you can take a shortcut by driving east on 36th Ave., which runs perpendicular between the two streets. At high tide, look for shorebird flocks that often roost in the fields in this area. Once on 72nd St., turn right and continue another 2.7 km (1.7 mi.) south to the parking area near the dyke. This immediate area is arguably one of the best places in North America in which to view large numbers of raptors of a variety of species, especially from October through March. Over a thousand Bald Eagles patrol this area in winter, along with good numbers of Red-tailed Hawk, Sharp-shinned Hawk, Cooper's Hawk, Merlin, and Peregrine Falcon. Gyrfalcon and Rough-legged Hawk are also present in winter, though only in ones and twos. Short-eared Owls are almost a guarantee around dusk, but they can be active throughout the day. The field immediately to the west of the parking lot (before the dyke) is worth a scan for hunting owls and raptors, both over the fields and along the powerlines and other perches. Once on the dyke, scan all the prominent logs, stumps, and shrubs around the flats and along the dyke. If Snowy Owls are around they should stick out quite conspicuously, but be aware of those tricky "plastic bag owls"! Stay on the dykes so as not to disturb hunting/roosting birds and the important grassland habitats that these raptors and other birds rely on.

The entire dyke pathway is paralleled by a number of ditches and bramble-patches. These thickets can be great for migrants in season, as well as sparrows and the odd warbler in winter (mainly Yellow-rumped Warbler with the odd Orange-crowned or Palm in some years). The shrubs and weedy patches along the dyke a few hundred metres/yards east of 72nd (adjacent to the Kings Links Golf Course) tend to be reliable spots for seeing American Tree Sparrows in winter, though they move around and aren't always close to the dyke. Listen for their high-pitched contact calls and check any flock of White-crowned Sparrows carefully.

If the tide is high, you should be able to scope a number of water birds on Boundary Bay, and the ponds on the golf course are also worth a scan. There are regularly several Eurasian Wigeon among the hundreds of American Wigeon that feed on the fairways and lounge in the ponds.

104TH ST. TO "THE MANSION" In recent years, this has been the most productive stretch of Boundary Bay for watching shorebirds on a rising tide (April–early May and late July–early November are the best periods for diversity, though there are usually a few over-summering birds and winter sees good numbers of Dunlin and Black-bellied Plovers). Since most birders visiting these sites will be targeting shorebirds, they are the focus of this section. Of the nearly fifty species recorded, here are some of the best finds from the area: Lesser Sand-Plover, Snowy Plover, Upland Sandpiper, Bristle-thighed Curlew, Far Eastern Curlew, Ruff, White-rumped Sandpiper, Red-necked Stint (adults are possibly annual in late July but only found if enough people are carefully checking through the Western Sandpiper flocks), and Little Stint.

It's best to arrive at least 1.5 hours before high tide; if the tide is out, most of the birds will be too far away to identify, and if it's all the way in, there's no shoreline for the birds to feed on. While a falling tide can be a fine time to visit, a rising tide is better, as it pushes the birds closer to you.

If you arrive during a low tide, you still have a chance of seeing a few birds out on the mudflats, and there are several spots close to the dyke that generally remain wet enough to attract a few shorebirds during low tides (namely the outflow channel at "The Mansion" west of 96th; see below).

To get to 104th, continue east along Ladner Trunk Rd. from 72nd, and turn right/south on Hornby Dr. at the first set of lights. DO NOT JOIN THE FREEWAY (Hwy. 99)! Hornby continues east and parallels Hwy. 99, giving access to 96th, 104th, and 112th Streets. Like 88th St. to the west, there's no "legal" place to park at the foot of 96th St., but some birders get away with stashing their car on the south side of the dyke where 96th meets the gravel jogging/bike path, then walking east or west. For obvious reasons I cannot condone this, so feel free to have a quick scan from the foot of 96th to see what's around, but then return to Hornby Dr. and head east to 104th where there's ample parking space at the end. From here you can walk or cycle east or west. It's a 2.6 km (1.6 mi.) walk/cycle (one way) from 104th west to The Mansion.

Once on the dyke, scan the mudflats in either direction to see if there are any conspicuous flocks around as this may determine which way you go. If there's nothing obvious to the east, proceed west back toward the foot of 96th St. (1.8 km/1.1 mi. one way). From August through early November, the wet weeds that have washed up close to the dyke attract flocks of Least, Baird's, and Pectoral Sandpipers. These birds can sometimes be found foraging here even during low tide. Check through these flocks carefully for Sharp-tailed Sandpiper and Buff-breasted Sandpiper (both annual in September–October). Closer to high tides, Western Sandpiper can also be common around the muddy pools along this stretch (outside of early summer and winter), along with other regular species mentioned in the overview. You'll see a set of old rotten pilings 1.2 km (¾ mi.) west of 104th. These are the remains of the East Delta Oyster Plant. Between 1940 and 1963, 50% of the provincial production of oysters came from Boundary Bay until water pollution made the local industry unfeasible. These ruins, known simply as "The Pilings" by local birders, are a great place to check for shorebirds taking shelter among the large chunks of wood. A freshwater seep here keeps the area fairly wet even at low tide, attracting both Yellowlegs species and many of the other freshwater-favouring species mentioned above.

From the foot of 96th St., it's another 800 m/yd. to the large house known to birders as "The Mansion" (we are so creative!). This spot can be well worth the walk thanks to an automated outflow channel that drains water from the surrounding farmland into the bay here. Species that prefer freshwater habitats, like yellowlegs and Long-billed Dowitchers, are regular here, and along with Reifel Refuge, it's one of the better spots in the Vancouver area for Stilt Sandpiper in August–September. Both Wilson's and Red-necked Phalaropes occasionally turn up in fall passage, many other species of shorebirds can be found here, and thousands of gulls use this outflow to bathe in after a long day at the dump. Also, scan any fallow fields on the other side of the dyke between here and 104th, as both Pacific and American Golden-Plovers can turn up in spring and fall for the lucky birder who scans carefully. For map, see page 69.

The "Sooty" subspecies of Fox Sparrow is one of the most common birds around Vancouver in winter. Listen for their loud *chuk* call notes coming from dense shrubs. MELISSA HAFTING

–11–

MAPLEWOOD FLATS, NORTH VANCOUVER

THERE WAS A time, not too long ago—maybe the 1990s or maybe even early 2000s—when if you asked someone what they thought of Maplewood Flats in North Vancouver, the standard response would be: "I don't know actually. I hear it's quite nice but I've never been." Admittedly, I grew up in the Okanagan Valley for the most part, which didn't help, but the first time I heard about Maplewood was around ten years ago. My Aunt Bette lived just down the road from it and figured it looked like a place where one might see a few birds. Auntie Bette was right.

With over 240 species recorded to date, the Maplewood Flats Conservation Area is undoubtedly one of the best year-round birding hotspots in BC, thanks to a wonderful diversity of habitats in a compact area. It offers the visitor a great sample of Pacific coast birds in all seasons, and thanks to regular patrols by dedicated locals, we now know it's a fantastic spot to be during songbird migration season. Unusual sightings from the past decade or so include Great Gray Owl, Lewis's Woodpecker, Ash-throated Flycatcher, Sage Thrasher, Tennessee Warbler, Black-and-White Warbler, and Chestnut-collared Longspur.

At the park headquarters, a whiteboard details recent sightings. This is where people meet for the free birding walks (10 am on the second Saturday of each month) by the Wild Bird Trust of BC. This is the same group that deserves credit for protecting and restoring the area, and turning it into the well-known spot that it is today.

In an era of constant urban expansion, it's refreshing to see little pockets like Maplewood flourishing just a stone's throw from the industrial dockyards of Vancouver and Burnaby. In the shadow of the North Shore Mountains, a visit to Maplewood at any time of year is sure to deliver your birding fix. Some corners of the park are quiet at times, but it's often a matter of finding the flock, then spending half an hour carefully checking each ball of feathers for something new.

BIRDING GUIDE

Note: *When using these directions, remember that the mountains are in the north.

From the office, take the trail that heads east toward the mudflats where good numbers of waterfowl and shorebirds can often be found in season (tides will also affect which

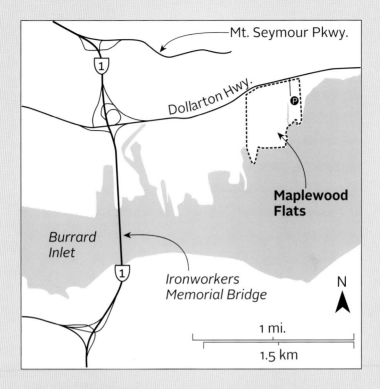

GETTING THERE

Take the Dollarton Hwy. exit (Exit 23) east off the Trans-Canada Hwy. (at the north end of the Ironworkers Memorial Bridge, also known as Second Narrows, across Burrard Inlet). Once on Dollarton, proceed 1.5 km (about 1 mi.) east. Look for access signs on the right side of the road, where you'll find the Wild Bird Trust office and parking. The park is accessible 24 hours from a walk-in gate just west of the driving entrance. The parking lot is open 6 am–6 pm Monday–Friday and 9:30 am–4 pm on weekends. It's usually closed on holidays. There's also parking on the north side of Dollarton on the gravel surrounding an ironworker's shop.

birds are around). In recent years, a Spotted Sandpiper has overwintered in this bay. From April into mid-summer, Purple Martins nest in the boxes set up on old pilings in the inlet. Nearly the entire North American population of this migratory species nests in structures built by volunteers, and Purple Martins are increasing yearly in coastal BC. Although they finish nesting in mid-summer, many of the birds hang around into late August/early September, so keep your eyes open for large swallow-like objects and listen for their distinctive chirps.

After checking the flats, head south toward the bridge where you can scan up the barge canal to the north. Continue across the bridge and take the right-hand trail, which leads westward toward the cattail ponds. The first pond is usually quiet, but the second is great for waterfowl and Virginia Rail in the spring, and occasionally Green Heron in summer. From there, head northward through the woodlot, which starts a loop trail; as you come through the woods, you'll end up on the west side of the west pond at a raised viewing area—another good place for Virginia Rail.

South of here are a meadow to your left/east and a salt marsh to your right. A little farther along, the trail branches again. The right branch takes you to what locals call Otter Point—at low tide a gravel bar is exposed, which attracts Black Oystercatcher among other things. Return to the main trail then turn left/east to head roughly back toward the footbridge. A pocket marsh on the left has produced Swamp Sparrow, Northern Waterthrush, Rusty Blackbird, and most recently—Palm Warbler. The trail heads eastward from there and follows the shore more or less back to the bridge.

The garden nursery as you entered the park is always worth a visit, especially in fall and winter when sparrows are attracted to several feeders that are set up. A walk along the Dollarton Hwy. to the east will bring you to a short trail at the mouth of McCartney Creek—the eastern boundary of the sanctuary. There's a small viewing deck there where American Dipper can sometimes be seen.

The grasslands of the Nicola Valley are the summer home of Swainson's Hawks, who migrate all the way to South America in winter. ILYA POVALYAEV

12

NICOLA VALLEY

HERE'S NO SHORTAGE of scenic routes in BC, but some are "birdier" than others. Hwy. 5A, or the old and slow way between Merritt and Kamloops, offers up a wonderful mélange of scenery and birding opportunities, and at a much more pleasant pace than the 120 km/hr zones on the main Hwy. 5.

Following a series of lakes and wetlands, and surrounded by the expansive dry grasslands of the Nicola Valley, this route provides a marvellous selection of nesting birds in summer, as well as migrant flocks during the shoulder seasons. Winter is certainly a quieter time, but even then there are still special birds to be found, including a good mix of raptors and the occasional Sharp-tailed Grouse feeding in roadside shrubs or budding trees.

This is one of the main routes into the Interior region and to the Rocky Mountains in Alberta. The route described below showcases the wonderful diversity of the Thompson and Nicola Valleys, as well as the rural beauty of the southern Interior.

BIRDING GUIDE

Nicola Lake is about 8.5 km (5.3 mi.) east of Merritt on Hwy. 5A. It's a relatively large lake—about 20 km (12.4 mi.) long—and provides great birding throughout the year, though things can slow down considerably if the lake is frozen. For a little side-trip and a great place to swim in summer, you can turn off to the left just before reaching the lake, following signs for Monck Park on the north side of the lake. Spring and fall are best for water birds, but even in mid-winter there are often ice-free areas on the lake. There are several spots where you can pull off the highway and scan for birds.

The Nicola River flows out of the lake at the very west end (near the Monck Park Rd. junction). There are usually a few (up to seven in winter) American Dippers and Barrow's Goldeneyes below the outlet dam, along with hundreds of dabbling ducks—mostly Mallards—in the shallows farther downstream. To check this out, turn off the highway onto the Nicola Cutoff Rd. just above the small Nicola Lake dam (first right after the Monck Park turnoff) and follow the road back down along the river to the start of the cattle feedlot, about 500 m/yd. downstream. The highway rest-stop about 4 km (2.5 mi.) east of the outlet is a good place to scan the water (from fall through spring) for Trumpeter Swans and

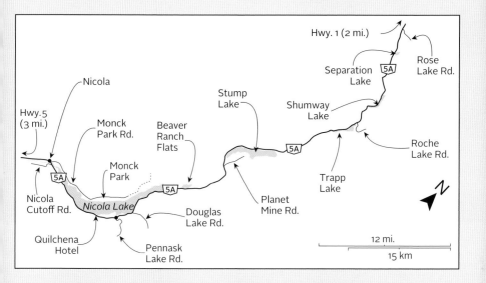

GETTING THERE

From Merritt or points south and west, look for signs for Kamloops but make sure to take the exit for Hwy. 5A north, which branches off near the airport and Walmart. Do not take Hwy. 5. From the Kamloops end, Hwy. 5A is well signed for Merritt near the top of the hill on Hwy. 97 (Exit 367) on the south side of Kamloops. Rose Hill Rd. will be on the left/east side of the highway, about 6 km (3.7 mi.) from the Kamloops junction of Hwys. 97 and 5A.

a variety of ducks, though the lake always freezes in winter in the shallow arm west of this point. Just as the Nicola Valley Golf Course appears on your right as you drive north, turn left (toward the lake) onto the unnamed gravel road, which briefly parallels the highway before reaching an obvious boat-launch. This is another great spot to scan the lake and check out the sandbar at the mouth of Quilchena Creek

Expansive grasslands cloak the hills around Beaver Ranch Flats on a crisp morning in the early spring. MURPHY SHEWCHUCK

just to the north. This turnoff is about 450 m/yd. southwest along the highway from the historic Quilchena Hotel. Continuing north toward Kamloops, the small bay at the base of the Pennask Lake Rd. is also worth a visit (first left after the Quilchena Hotel). A short section of the old highway (obvious on the lake side) a few hundred metres/yards farther on also provides scoping opportunities of the lake and adjacent marshes.

The Nicola River flows into the lake about 13 km (8 mi.) farther north (about 1.5 km/1 mi. north of the Douglas Lake Rd. junction). This is a great place to check in spring and fall for waterfowl, grebes, loons, and gulls; pull off just south of the bridge and scan the beach. American Tree Sparrows can be found in the shrubbery here in winter.

Just 3.5 km (2.2 mi.) north of Nicola Lake on Hwy. 5A is Beaver Ranch Flats (also known as Guichon Flats), a Ducks Unlimited project that's one of the finest birding spots in the province. There's a parking area on the west side of the highway. Birding is best from mid-March through November, with highlights including large colonies of Eared Grebes, Black Terns, and Yellow-headed Blackbirds. Also breeding here are many species of ducks, Wilson's Phalaropes, and sometimes American Avocets. In the late spring of 2015, several White-faced Ibises took up residency and consequently attracted a number of birders. In the spring and fall, large numbers of water birds use the marsh as a staging area, including flocks of Tundra Swans, Sandhill Cranes, American White Pelicans, and a variety of shorebirds. Finally, scan the dry hillsides on the opposite side of the marsh (directly across from the parking area) for Burrowing Owls. A small colony was reintroduced here in the 1990s, and many of the adults return each year to nest. Under the new ABA rules, this population is considered countable since they are a native species and have established a successful breeding population in the wild. Dusk is the best time to see the birds hunting, but at any time of day, look for them perched up on rocks, posts, or piles of rocks.

As you proceed north, watch for Lewis's Woodpeckers in the open pine woods along the highway between here and Stump Lake (about 9 km/5.6 mi. north), with the most reliable area being in the pine snags along the Planet Mine Rd., which turns off to the right roughly 7 km (4.3 mi.) north of Beaver Ranch Flats. If you're travelling from the north, it's the first left after Stump Lake.

Stump Lake is always worth a stop from spring through fall; the best pull-offs are at the sound end and about halfway along the western lakeshore. This lake has particularly large numbers of ducks, grebes, and coots during fall migration.

Just over 14 km (8.7 mi.) north of Stump Lake, immediately after passing Trapp Lake (usually not very productive but still worth a scan for water birds in season), is the signed turnoff for Roche Lake Provincial Park. This is outside the scope of this chapter, but if you're looking for a mixture of great forest and wetland habitats plus camping opportunities, it's certainly worth a visit.

Continue north from the Roche Lake junction, passing Shumway Lake. After 13.5 km (8.4 mi.), the small Separation Lake will appear on the right side (from the north, it's 3.4 km/2.1 mi. south of Rose Hill). There's a dirt track at the north end of the lake from which you can scope for shorebirds and waterfowl. April–May and August–October are the best times for variety, but Barrow's Goldeneye, Eared Grebes, and Wilson's Phalaropes are some of the highlights that stay to breed in most years. Western Kingbird, Say's Phoebe, Mountain Bluebird, Savannah and Vesper Sparrows, and Western Meadowlark all nest nearby, and a smaller pond just north of the lake (accessed via the same ranch road) can produce a few additional water bird species. Swainson's Hawk, Red-tailed Hawk, Northern Harrier, and American Kestrel all breed in this area, while Rough-legged Hawks appear in winter, and Ferruginous Hawks have been sighted on several occasions. This is one of the best places in the Kamloops area to see migrating Sandhill Cranes by the thousands. Spring migration usually peaks around April 20; fall migration peaks September 21–30.

Return to Hwy. 5A, proceed north for 3.6 km (2.2 mi.), then turn right on Rose Hill Rd. In early spring, this is a great road for grassland birds such as Swainson's Hawk, Long-billed Curlew, Mountain Bluebird, Horned Lark, Vesper Sparrow, and Western Meadowlark. Snow Buntings pass through regularly in late fall and early spring; they also winter in the general area but have become scarce in recent years for unknown reasons. Snowy Owls (rare in the Interior) are nearly annual in winter. Grasslands in this area are also good places to hear Lapland Longspurs in migration, but seeing them is often a challenge. Commanding vistas from hilltops in this area make for excellent raptor viewing during the spring and fall migrations. Land on either side of the road is private but unfenced in some areas, so be aware of your surroundings.

The French name for the Common Yellowthroat is "paruline masque" (Masked Warbler)—which is a much better name for this energetic wetland denizen. The "witchity-witchity" song often serves as the soundtrack to a summer visit to Salmon Arm Bay. MELISSA HAFTING

—13—

SALMON ARM BAY

WITH CLOSING IN on 300 species recorded in its history, there's a legitimate case to call Salmon Arm Bay the best single birding site in BC. Coastal birders will protest, but as any visitor from spring through fall will attest, there are A LOT of birds along the waterfront of Salmon Arm, and thanks to the efforts of dedicated local birders (namely Ted Hillary and Don Cecile), an impressive list has been amassed, including some impressive rarities such as Snowy Egret, White-tailed Kite, Little Gull, Pomarine Jaeger, White Wagtail, Bay-breasted Warbler, and numerous shorebirds of note (see below).

Located along the Trans-Canada Hwy., Salmon Arm is a convenient birding stop for people travelling from the coast to the Rocky Mountains, or for anyone wanting to see a great variety of water birds. The annual Salmon Arm Grebe Festival is held each May to celebrate BC's largest colony of Western Grebes (the only other colony being on Duck Lake in Creston). In addition to the hundred or so pairs of Western Grebes, there are usually good numbers of Red-necked and Pied-billed Grebes breeding in the area, as well as one to three pairs of Clark's Grebes. In spring and fall, it's usually possible to see a few Horned Grebes (most numerous in winter), as well as the odd Eared Grebe.

Salmon Arm's other claim to fame is its freshwater mudflats, which attract a bounty of shorebirds in late summer and early fall. When the conditions are right, Salmon Arm Bay can be the best shorebirding spot in BC's Interior. Many species of shorebirds pass through in spring, but the water is often too high to expose enough foraging habitat. From late July into November, the entire shoreline of Salmon Arm Bay is worth checking (especially the southwest corner where the Salmon River empties into the lake). At least thirty-six species of shorebird have been recorded in the Bay, including local rarities like Pacific Golden-Plover, Upland Sandpiper, Buff-breasted Sandpiper (nearly annual), Black Turnstone, Surfbird, Sharp-tailed Sandpiper, and Red Phalarope. The location of shorebird flocks can vary daily, and will depend on exposed mud. In most years there isn't extensive mud until late August, with September being the best month to expect big numbers of sandpipers.

BIRDING GUIDE

There are three main access points to view the bay, all of which are worth checking no matter the time of year or the lake level.

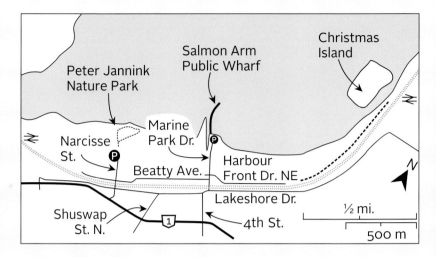

Christmas Island

Salmon Arm Public Wharf

Peter Jannink Nature Park

Marine Park Dr.

Narcisse St.

Beatty Ave.

Harbour Front Dr. NE

Lakeshore Dr.

½ mi.

Shuswap St. N.

4th St.

500 m

GETTING THERE

Salmon Arm is located along the Trans-Canada Hwy. (Hwy. 1), 109 km (68 mi.) east of Kamloops and 461 km (286 mi.) from Vancouver. It's a convenient stop for anyone travelling between Vancouver and the Rocky Mountains or Calgary, and the Okanagan Valley is just a short drive to the south.

SALMON ARM PUBLIC WHARF The best place to view the grebes is from the Salmon Arm Public Wharf located at the end of Marine Park Dr. From Hwy. 1, turn north onto 4th St. (following the binocular signs); drive two blocks to Lakeshore Dr., turn right, then make an immediate left across the railway tracks onto Marine Park Dr. Park on the right, then you can walk out onto the wharf. At any time of year there should be lots of waterfowl to look at (unless the bay is frozen). The Western Grebes will be spread out to the east and west during the nesting season. To see a Clark's you'll probably need a scope—look for a bird with pale silvery flanks, an all-white face with eyes distinctly separate from the cap, and a bright orange bill that's often visible even at great distances.

PETER JANNINK NATURE PARK The wharf can be a good place to scan for shorebirds in season but typically this spot is even better. From the Salmon Arm wharf parking area, head back along Marine Park Dr., then turn right on Beatty Ave. (before the railway tracks). Continue roughly westward for 600 m/yd. then turn right onto Narcisse St. Park at the end of the road near the gate and walk in. There's a nice gazebo here, and the brushy habitat on the west side of the park can be good for migrant songbirds in spring and fall. Straight out from the gazebo you'll be able to scope the lakeshore and an adjacent wetland to the east. A walking path that leads along the lakeshore back toward the wharf provides more views of the marshes. For those wanting closer looks at the shorebirds in fall, it's okay to cross the fence at the northwest corner of the park then walk out onto the shoreline—but bring your boots and tread carefully as the mud can be deep and predatory in places. Also, keep a respectable distance from the birds so as not to disturb them at this important staging time in their migration.

CHRISTMAS ISLAND Located in the southeast corner of Salmon Arm Bay, Christmas Island (named after Eric Christmas, one of the key people involved in reserving the Salmon Arm foreshore as a bird sanctuary) is an artificial island (constructed from earth dredged up while making the marina) that's simply a great place for birds. Perhaps the most conspicuous residents are the hundreds of Ring-billed Gulls who have established BC's largest Ring-billed Gull breeding colony here. A good mix of waterfowl will usually be on show, as well as a number of different shorebirds in late summer and early fall. To get there from the public wharf, drive back toward the railway tracks, turn left/east onto Harbour Front Dr., and take this all the way to the end. Park in the small parking area and walk along the track to the north. The bushes and trees along the trail are great for migrants in spring and fall, and have been particularly good for sparrows in September/October with notable finds such as American Tree, Harris's, and Swamp Sparrows. Once out toward the island (accessible by foot unless water levels are high), you'll notice a couple viewing platforms for better looks at birds along the shoreline and out on the lake.

—14—

BEAVER LAKE ROAD, LAKE COUNTRY

THIS HAS LONG been a favourite birding area for Central Okanaganites and it's swiftly gaining a province-wide reputation for its tremendous habitat diversity along a relatively short stretch of road. Beginning in downtown Winfield, north of Kelowna, Beaver Lake Rd. passes a small industrial area before climbing up through expansive grasslands with scattered Ponderosa Pines, providing fine views of the Lake Country municipality. As the road winds higher into the hills, thick aspen copses begin to appear along creeks, then the forest thickens into a mixture

◄ Fortunately for birders, the Northern Pygmy-Owl is diurnal, which means that it defends its territory and hunts for prey during daylight hours. As you explore the forested sections of Beaver Lake Rd., keep an eye out for suspicious blobs near the tops of trees, and listen for its repeated *toot* calls. MELISSA HAFTING

of Douglas Fir, Ponderosa Pine, and even Western Red Cedar before turning into boreal forest as you approach Beaver Lake itself. Not only can the visiting birder expect to encounter a wonderful mix of southern Interior specialties like Dusky Flycatcher, Western Kingbird, Say's Phoebe, Pygmy Nuthatch, White-breasted Nuthatch, Western Bluebird, Mountain Bluebird, Lazuli Bunting, and Cassin's Finch, but since the drive from Hwy. 97 to Beaver Lake Lodge is less than 15 km (9.3 mi.), you'll soon be in upper-elevation forest that has Spruce Grouse, American Three-toed Woodpecker, Boreal Chickadee, and Pine Grosbeak practically year-round.

Hawk migration-watching can be very productive here under good conditions in March–April and September–November. There are multiple spring records of Ferruginous Hawk as well as Broad-winged Hawk in August-September, so pay close attention for that species.

In winter the road is quieter but still worth a visit—especially for the upper-elevation specialties. The road is plowed regularly during the snowy months and should be driveable to the Beaver Lake Lodge for most vehicles, although winter tires are recommended and you should take it slow when returning down the hill.

BIRDING GUIDE

The distance markings along this road are fairly inconsistent, so instead of worrying about looking for inconspicuous or missing yellow signs on the roadside, simply proceed east past Winfield's industrial buildings. When you get to the last large building with all the waterslide parts stacked up on the right side, zero your odometer—this is just where the

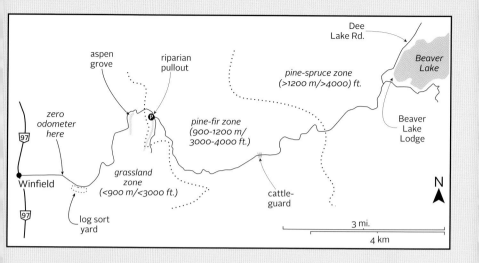

GETTING THERE

Beaver Lake Rd. is well signed off Hwy. 97 in downtown Winfield (just north of the Kelowna airport). From the south, it's the first major intersection after passing Duck Lake (Ellison Lake) on the right side. From the north, it's about 3.8 km (2.4 mi.) south of the Oceola Rd. turnoff, right at the south end of Wood Lake. Look for the Shell gas station and turn east (west will put you on the Glenmore Rd.), toward the extensive grassy hills in the distance. Follow the straight Beaver Lake Rd. through an industrial area then zero your odometer at the bottom of the hill as instructed above.

road begins to climb a hill. As you pass through this industrial sector and continue up the hill past a small log-sorting operation, check the fencelines and other structures for Say's Phoebe from March through August.

Continuing up through the grassland, you'll notice nestboxes on some fence posts. These are used annually by both Western and Mountain Bluebird, and Tree and Violet-green

Swallows. The songs of Vesper Sparrows and Western Meadowlarks highlight spring and summer mornings, while the occasional Clay-coloured Sparrow may set up territory in patches of rose thickets in some years. Swainson's and Red-tailed Hawks soar above the grasslands in summer, while Rough-legged Hawks replace Swainson's in winter. Golden Eagle is also possible here year-round along with the more common Bald Eagle and ever-present American Kestrels. Northern Shrikes may be spotted on prominent perches in October–April, and lucky birders may run into migrant flocks of Horned Larks or Snow Buntings in early spring or late fall.

Stop when you come to an obvious line of aspens with thick underbrush, just where the road swings left—about 3.4 km (2.1 mi.) from where you zeroed your odometer. This line of shrubs and small trees can be productive for songbirds in migration and yields a number of quality birds during the breeding season such as Red-naped Sapsucker, Calliope Hummingbird, Rufous Hummingbird, Red-eyed Vireo, Least Flycatcher, Eastern Kingbird, House Wren, Gray Catbird, Nashville Warbler, MacGillivray's Warbler, Spotted Towhee, and Lazuli Bunting. In summer 2014, a Black-billed Cuckoo sang here for at least a week.

In another 800 m/yd., park at the obvious pull-out on the right side near some large Ponderosa Pines. The riparian grove below the road on the right/south side can produce many of the species previously mentioned but also check the pines for mixed flocks of nuthatches (all three species are possible here year-round) and Cassin's Finch outside of winter. Cassin's, Warbling, and Red-eyed Vireo all nest in the area, and Ruffed Grouse is commonly heard displaying in spring and fall. Look for Clark's Nutcrackers on the tops of pines, and look and listen for the diurnal Northern Pygmy-Owl. During migration periods, especially May, it's often productive to walk along the road from here in both directions, as you never know what you might run into in these roadside bushes. Dusky Grouse occurs in the open forest here but can be quite elusive at the best of times.

Continue another 4.1 km (2.5 mi.) from the pull-out to a cattle-guard at the bottom of a steep hill. You can stop in between, but keep to the road as most of the land is private here. Once at the site described above, bird the mixed forest on either side of the road as it heads straight up the hill from the cattle-guard. The birches and aspens are particularly good for Red-naped Sapsucker from late March through August and Ruffed Grouse are often near the roadside here. Both Dusky and Hammond's Flycatchers can be found here, providing a tricky identification challenge, with other common songsters in summer including Townsend's Solitaire, Townsend's Warbler, and Western Tanager. In winter, check the birches for Common Redpoll flocks, which have occasionally included Hoary Redpoll in the past.

From here it's roughly 5 km (3.1 mi.) to the top of the hill where Beaver Lake Lodge is signed on the right. As you start to see Lodgepole Pine and Engelmann Spruce replace the Douglas Fir forest, your chances for upper-elevation specialties like Spruce Grouse, American Three-toed Woodpecker, Black-backed Woodpecker, Gray Jay, Boreal Chickadee, Pine Grosbeak, and White-winged Crossbill really kick in (the latter two being most frequent in winter, especially in good spruce cone crop years). For an even better chance at many of these species, continue to the left along Dee Lake Rd., which you can take all the way to Hwy. 6 east of Vernon (about 40 km/25 mi. along logging roads), but much of the best habitat is between Beaver Lake and Dee Lake. These roads are beyond the scope of this chapter, so take a backroads map or check directions online before attempting them.

In winter, the main mountain roads are plowed regularly, but watch for logging trucks and find safe pull-outs whenever you stop. Boreal Owl is possible along the Dee Lake Rd. with the most vocal times being January–April and September–November. Like Boreal Chickadees, they prefer areas with extensive Subalpine Fir, particularly near boggy wetlands. During the summer, common forest birds in the highlands here include Olive-sided Flycatcher, Dusky Flycatcher, Pacific Wren, Ruby-crowned Kinglet, Hermit Thrush, American Robin, Varied Thrush, Golden-crowned Kinglet, Yellow-rumped Warbler, Orange-crowned Warbler, Wilson's Warbler, Northern Waterthrush, Dark-eyed Junco, Fox Sparrow, Song Sparrow, and Lincoln's Sparrow.

15

WHITE LAKE, SOUTH OKANAGAN

W HEN VISITING THE Okanagan you may hear people talk about how it's a "semi-desert" or that it's the northern end of the Sonoran Desert, hence the abundance of rattlesnakes, prickly-pear cactus, and sweaty birders. From a habitat perspective, the South Okanagan is technically shrub-steppe and not a desert, meaning that annual rainfall is comparable to a desert's (Osoyoos gets less precipitation than Tombstone, Arizona!) but cooler winters allow the ground to retain more moisture, thus the abundance of grasses, sagebrush, rabbit brush, and antelope brush instead of saguaro cactus and barren earth.

The South Okanagan's unique climate and habitats support flora and fauna found nowhere else in Canada,

The Brewer's Sparrow might be the definition of an "LBJ" (Little Brown Job), but its boisterous song and limited Canadian breeding range make it a top target for birders visiting the sagebrush grasslands of White Lake. LIRON GERTSMAN

including a number of threatened and endangered species. Since the majority of these rare species occur in the native grasslands and dry shrub-steppe country, I had to include at least one representative site in this book. Picking just one was a challenge, but I settled on White Lake due to its convenient accessibility, as well as my intimate knowledge of the place from my childhood spent chasing salamanders and searching out rare insects, to my first paid birding job studying bluebirds and swallows, then later as a member of a Canadian Wildlife Service team researching Brewer's Sparrows and Sage Thrashers.

BIRDING GUIDE

From the north (driving south along White Lake Rd. from Penticton), stop at the turnoff for the Dominion Radio Astrophysical Observatory on the left side of the road where the valley opens up and trees dissipate into expansive sage brush grassland. Park near the information kiosk and assess your surroundings. Lark Sparrows nest near this spot most summers and Vesper Sparrows are abundant throughout the area. Lazuli Buntings are also in the area and you may note either Mountain or Western Bluebirds nesting in the boxes along the fenceline. Western Meadowlarks are common throughout the grasslands March–October, and this spot can be a good place to hear Common Poorwill at night in May–September.

About 700 m/yd. beyond the observatory turnoff, the Fairview–White Lake Rd. turns off to the left/south. Continuing straight will take you to the community of Twin Lakes and Hwy. 3A near Yellow Lake. The first 3 km (about 2 mi.)

offer similar habitat to that of White Lake, and occasionally Sage Thrashers can be found singing along this road. The first buildings on the left are the old headquarters of the White Lake Ranch. The fields around here can be good to scan for Gray Partridge and families of Dusky Grouse in summer. The copses of aspen that come close to the road on the left side can have Least Flycatcher and Red-naped Sapsucker in summer, and Lazuli Bunting is common here, as are both species of bluebirds.

To reach White Lake, turn left/south onto the Fairview–White Lake Rd. There's a bit of a wide spot on the left just as you start going down the hill, allowing you views of the lake. Park along this slight pull-off area (watch for oncoming traffic), and walk to the fenceline on the east side so you can scan your surroundings. Most of the biggest sagebrush is in this area, so it's the most reliable zone to find the semi-colonial Brewer's Sparrow (mostly concentrated between the top of the hill and the lake), and also (currently) the most reliable site in Canada to find Sage Thrasher (mid-May–August). The surrounding land is all owned by the Nature Trust, so you're permitted to cross the fence and explore as you see fit. Cactus and rattlesnakes are common here, so wear proper footwear and watch where you step. In the past, the grassy flats at the north end of the lake have had nesting Long-billed Curlews, but in recent years they've only been seen on migration. The lake itself can be good for shorebirds and waterfowl in spring and fall, but if it's dry you'll see nothing but white salt-pan (hence the name).

Anywhere in the area can produce Gray Partridge, but sometimes they take many hours of trudging around before one is lucky enough to flush them. They can sometimes be

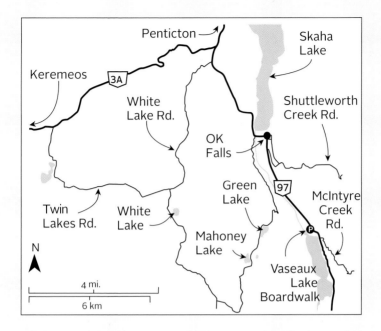

GETTING THERE

White Lake is located near the north end of the Fairview–White Lake Rd. From Penticton, turn right/east onto White Lake Rd., 500 m/yd. south of the Hwy. 3A turnoff, then take the first left after passing the Dominion Radio Astrophysical Observatory. From the main intersection in downtown Oliver, head southwest from the 7-Eleven past the high school along Fairview Rd., then turn right to head north on the Fairview–White Lake Rd. and follow it all the way until you get into the obvious sagebrush basin of White Lake.

seen along the roadside in the early morning. For one of the more reliable areas, drive down the hill and park at the pull-off on the right side where the road bends just west of the lake. Here there's a cattle-gate and an old driving track heading up the hill to the southwest. On the opposite side of the road, note the thick patches of weeds along the roadside. These can be great for migrating sparrows, including American Tree Sparrow. Go through the gate and zigzag along the old track until it fizzles out. There's plenty of room to explore in search of partridges and other grassland birds. This area west of the road is usually the best zone for Grasshopper Sparrows. Look and listen for them in more extensive areas of bunchgrass to the west of the rounded hills and toward the White Lake Ranch buildings. Also note that there's a small basin to the north of here that sometimes fills up with water. This can be a good spot for a few shorebirds in migration, though more often it's a great spot for migrating American Pipits that feed in the wet mud. More unusual but still annual, Snow Buntings, Lapland Longspurs, and Horned Larks can all be encountered in this area—especially if you know their calls.

For a nice walk and an easy way to get close to the lake, continue south past the lake to an obvious parking area with an obvious track leading north back toward the lake. Both bluebird species may be nesting in the boxes along the fence, while White-throated Swifts can be seen chattering overhead. Nashville Warbler, Western Tanager, Spotted Towhee, and Chipping Sparrow are some of the species that may be heard singing near the base of the cliffs in summer, and look for Say's Phoebes at the old wooden corral near the lake. Brewer's Sparrows and Sage Thrashers can also be found in this area, though they're usually more numerous on the west side of the lake. Continuing straight past the corral will take you along the east side of the lake and eventually to the border of the observatory property. Otherwise, you can turn right at the corral and follow the track up the hill past some small ponds and into lovely open pine forest. This trail goes all the way over to Mahoney Lake on the Green Lake Rd. and can be a great half-day hike for encountering Okanagan birds, including a very slim chance for White-headed Woodpecker.

From the parking area south of the lake, you can continue south along Fairview–White Lake Rd. past a shallow wetland on the left (often good for all three teal species in spring), before heading down a hill and back into pine forest, and eventually to the small community of Willowbrook, where you can either return the way you came, turn left onto the Green Lake Rd. to get to Okanagan Falls, or continue south to Oliver.

Diversity is highest in April–September. Winter is a very quiet time at White Lake but it's still a pleasant place to visit and Gray Partridge are often easier to find when snow is on the ground. In winter, White Lake is usually one of the more reliable sites to find Rough-legged Hawk and Northern Shrike.

Like the other members of their family, White-throated Swifts are most often high in the sky. On some days though, lucky birders can be treated to eye-level views of these cliff-nesting speedsters, as they chatter and swoop above the grasslands overlooking Vaseux Lake. LIRON GERTSMAN

16

VASEUX LAKE, SOUTH OKANAGAN

O F THE MAJOR lakes that line the Canadian side of the Okanagan Valley from north to south, Vaseux Lake (from the French for "muddy water") is the only one that bans motorized boats. The entire lake is a wild-life refuge, and the rich wetlands and riparian habitats that fringe it, especially at the north end, are critical for a range of migratory, breeding, and wintering birds that visit the valley each year. An estimated 85% of the Okanagan's wetlands have been lost over the years due to urban and agricultural development, making sites like Vaseux Lake even more important. Given its close proximity to the rocky cliffs and dry hillsides of pine forest and grassland, the diversity of species found here is impressive, particularly for those "Okanagan specials" (birds found nowhere else in Canada but the Okanagan and adjacent valleys) such as Chukar, White-throated Swift, Lewis's Woodpecker, Black-chinned Hummingbird, Gray Flycatcher, Canyon Wren, and Pygmy Nuthatch.

I'll limit this account to the north end of the lake, truly one of the best areas in the Okanagan, and indeed the province, to amass a wonderful birding list in a short time, all in a tremendous setting with other interesting wildlife possible, such as California Bighorn Sheep.

This area is worth a visit at any time of year, but like most Interior sites, late spring and early summer, when birds are singing joyfully and the mornings are still cool, provide some of the most enjoyable birding opportunities. If you're visiting in August/September, drop by the Vaseux Lake Bird Observatory (see below) for a chance to see birds in the hand as they're captured in mist-nets, carefully extracted, then measured and banded for future identification if re-netted.

In winter, the lake is often mostly frozen, though there is usually some open water near the north end where wintering swans of both species (mostly Trumpeter with a few Tundra) are joined by a variety of other water birds. For the best waterfowl diversity, visit in late fall and early spring. Summer is a quiet time for birds on the lake itself, but all three teal species (Cinnamon, Blue-winged, and Green-winged) nest in the area, as do Red-necked and Pied-billed Grebes, Redhead and other more common species.

BIRDING GUIDE

Whenever I visit Vaseux Lake, I like to start by driving up the McIntyre Creek Rd. to a wide pull-out from which you

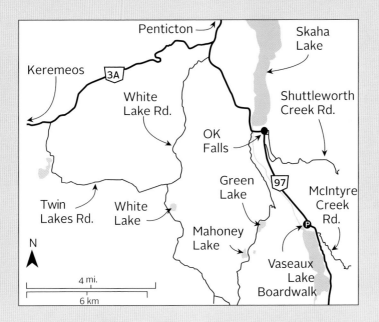

GETTING THERE

Vaseux Lake is conveniently located along Hwy. 97, around a 20 minute drive south of Penticton, or 12 minutes north of Oliver.

can scan almost the entire lake while you listen and look for rocky-country birds around the cliffs above you. To reach this road (confusingly labelled Dulton Creek Rd. on Google Maps and known locally as Irrigation Creek Rd.), look for the gravel road on the east (cliff) side of Hwy. 97, just 400 m/yd. south of the signed Vaseux Wildlife Centre parking area at the north end of the lake, or just over 100 m north of the lakeside provincial park camping area. Once on the gravel road, proceed another 750 m/yd. and park at the wide pull-off where the road swings to the left.

Spring is the most popular season to visit Road 22, especially on the long weekend in May when ambitious birders take part in the annual Okanagan Big Day Challenge—a race to see as many species as possible in 24 hours.
RICHARD CANNINGS

You may want to stop beforehand and explore the cliffs and adjacent grassland. Canyon Wrens and Chukar can be found in this area throughout the year, while White-throated Swift and Rock Wren nest in summer. Sunny mornings are generally the best time to hear and possibly see these birds. At the pull-out, you can set up a scope and scan the lake for water birds. This is also a great viewpoint to look for soaring raptors, including Golden Eagles and Peregrine Falcons— both local nesters. In the middle of the S-bend here (where you parked) as you approach the cliffs, notice a walking track that heads roughly north up a slight hill at the base of a large boulder field. This is a great way to get close to the rocky habitat where the wrens and Chukar can be found.

Look for the Aboriginal pictographs on a large rock (made from ochre originating from a site near Princeton) which are likely several hundred years old (certainly pre-European contact). Be very wary of poison ivy and rattlesnakes in this area and watch where you step. Prickly pear cactus is also common. If you drive farther up the road, turn around near the farmhouse and check each pine snag carefully for Lewis's Woodpecker (May–September) as several pairs nest along this road. Other common breeders of note here are Violet-green Swallow, Western Kingbird, Western Wood-Pewee, Clark's Nutcracker, House Wren, Spotted Towhee, and Lazuli Bunting. Though scarcer than Chukar, Gray Partridge also occur in the grasslands here.

Return to the highway and turn right then make an immediate left into the gravel parking lot at the north end of Vaseux Lake. There are pit-toilets and picnic tables here, but the main attraction is the boardwalk trail that heads out to a two-storey public viewing hide. You'll pass through willow and birch thickets, home to nesting Willow Flycatcher, Veery, Yellow Warbler, Black-headed Grosbeak, and Bullock's Oriole in summer, and several oxbow sloughs where you might hear chattering Marsh Wrens or calling Sora and Virginia Rail. What you see from the viewing platform will vary greatly throughout the year, with winter and migration periods being the most interesting times to visit. If the water is low enough, a sandbar is exposed, providing ample habitat for resting gulls, terns, and shorebirds in season.

Finally, the Vaseux Lake Bird Observatory and its surrounding trails are worth a visit at any time of year (but the observatory is typically only operational from August 1 into early October). To reach it, return to Hwy. 97, turn left/ north and proceed 1 km (0.6 mi.) to a pull-out area on the left side of the road. There's a gate here with an old track heading down the hill past an oxbow of the Okanagan River. *Do not confuse this with the more obvious pull-off area a little farther north where there's no track leading down to the wetland/riparian area. When you get to the bottom of the slight hill, the trail splits to the left and right. Heading left will take you along a line of birches and willows that hug the oxbow for several hundred metres. There's also a small pond that you can sometimes see from the trail. Expect many of the usual wetland and riparian birds here (including Yellow-breasted Chat in spring/late summer), and it can be a good spot for migrating songbirds in spring and fall. Heading right will eventually take you out to the dyke along the Okanagan River channel. Once on the dyke you can walk a little ways north before a rose thicket blocks your path, or you can head south almost to the outlet into Vaseux Lake. While this area can be relatively quiet on some days, even during migration, there have been some remarkable records over the years, including Green Heron, Boreal Owl, Black-capped Vireo, Chestnut-sided Warbler, Prothonotary Warbler, Le Conte's Sparrow, and Indigo Bunting. For map, see page 111.

17

ROAD 22,
SOUTH OKANAGAN

WHILE ROAD 22 itself runs between Hwy. 97 and Black Sage Rd., just north of Osoyoos and south of Oliver, the birding area known as Road 22 is generally considered to encompass all the fields, marshes, oxbows, woodland, and scrub habitats to the north and south of the road between Hwy. 97 and Black Sage Rd. (to the west and east respectively), as well as similar habitats adjacent to the four river dyke trails that run 1.5 km (0.9 mi.) south to Osoyoos Lake, and 2.3 km (1.4 mi.) to the first drop-structure/footbridge north of the Road 22 bridge. There are patches of similar habitats to the north, but those are outside of the scope of this chapter. Visitors will no doubt notice the large old barn and old farmhouse at the east end of Road 22.

In the Okanagan, Yellow-breasted Chat habitat is often associated with rose-thickets, stinging nettle, and poison ivy. Therefore it is much more preferable to wait patiently for a singing bird to perch up like this! LIRON GERTSMAN

These are some of the last remains of the old Haynes Ranch that once covered much of the South Okanagan (over 20,000 acres-worth, or close to 9,000 hectares). Valentine Haynes, the son of John Haynes who founded the ranch, is reported to have been the first Caucasian child born in the South Okanagan, in 1875. The ranch was used as a cattle ranch, and boasted 4,200 head at its peak. Ownership of the land has changed and been divided up quite a bit over the years, and today the Nature Trust manages most of the pasture and oxbow lands on either side of the Okanagan River near Road 22. Therefore, the public is permitted to leave the dykes that run north and south of Road 22 to explore the woodlots. However, be aware that local cattlemen still lease the area to run their stock, so fence-jumpers should be wary of temperamental bulls. It's also important to know that poison ivy is extremely abundant in the forest here and can cause a rash even in winter when the leaves are gone.

Road 22 has something to offer any time of year, but if you had to pick one season to visit, spring is the easy answer—particularly in the middle of May when songbird migration is at its peak, shorebirds and waterfowl are still moving through (especially if some of the fields are flooded), and local breeding specialties like Yellow-breasted Chat and Bobolink are setting up territories.

BIRDING GUIDE

Depending on what direction you are coming from, the order in which you visit the different areas of Road 22 will vary.

Beginning at the junction of Hwy. 97 and Road 22, check the wetland near the cattle-guard for rails, blackbirds, and

Marsh Wren; if there's enough water you may spy Wilson's Phalaropes foraging along the ditches. Wilson's Snipes are common, and males are often seen perching on the fence-posts close to the road. As you move east beyond the first marsh, the fields open up; these are worth scanning for curlews in spring and Bobolinks from mid-May into August. A small pond in front of one of the houses can sometimes yield a surprising variety of ducks and the odd shorebird, so scan it carefully. As you wind along an S-bend and start approaching the Road 22 bridge over the river, pull into the gravel parking lot on the south side of the road. A kiosk notes the importance of the expansive fields for Bobolinks. Numbers have declined since new houses went in during the mid-2000s, and Bobolink nests can be destroyed if the hay is harvested too early, so it's a tenuous existence for these South American migrants. This parking lot is also a great place to scan for curlews that often nest in the same fields as the Bobolink, and there are almost always a few Northern Harriers hunting nearby. In winter this spot offers a great vantage point for scanning for hawks and eagles in all directions.

At the bridge you'll notice that four river-dykes head north and south on either side of the Okanagan River. Generally the only dyke open for vehicle traffic is the southeast dyke (see below). The other dykes are always open to pedestrians and all offer good birding potential throughout the year. If you want to do a loop walk to the north, note that the next bridge across the Okanagan River channel is 2.3 km (1.4 mi.) upstream.

Of the four quadrants of Road 22, the woodlands and marshes along the driveable southeast dyke are probably the

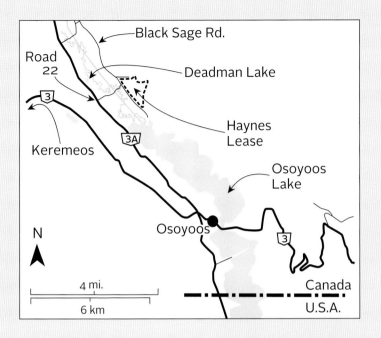

GETTING THERE

From Osoyoos, Road 22 is signed on the right/east side of Hwy. 97, 7.7 km (4.8 mi.) north of the big Husky gas station at the Hwy. 3 junction. From the main intersection in downtown Oliver, Road 22 is 12.2 km (7.6 mi.) south along Hwy. 97. Another option for those driving to and from Oliver is to drive south on the Black Sage Rd.: From the main intersection in Oliver, turn east (follow signs for Mount Baldy Ski Area), then look for Black Sage on the right immediately after passing the Petro-Can gas station. This slower but more scenic route will take you to the east end of Road 22 (at the old barn). It's also possible to cycle/walk all the way along the river dyke between the town of Oliver and Road 22 (11.5 km/7 mi. one-way), which makes for a fun day trip.

hardest to penetrate on foot (and are filled with poison ivy and stinging nettle). Therefore, it's highly advisable to stick to the track. As you start out south, there's a weedy field immediately on the left/east—a great area for sparrows in fall and winter. Farther along, the thick riparian woodland will come closer to the road where two oxbows border on the dyke. These are great spots during spring migration when warblers are moving through. In the breeding season Yellow-breasted Chats are common here; and listen for Bewick's Wren and Least Flycatcher among the more abundant birds like Western Wood-Pewee, Yellow Warbler, Black-headed Grosbeak, and American Goldfinch. Approach the oxbows carefully and check for Wood Duck, Gadwall, and all three teal species in summer. Soon another pasture with a tall radio tower will come up on the left. Bobolinks and Long-billed Curlews are sometimes present in this field, and Ospreys will be conspicuous on their nesting platforms. In winter, this is a great place to be at dusk, when hundreds of blackbirds return from a day's foraging at a local cattle feedlot near the Oliver landfill. Typically, around 3:45 pm onward they fly in and sit on the wires before roosting in the marsh. Red-winged and Brewer's Blackbirds make up the vast majority of the flock, but careful eyes can often pick up a Rusty Blackbird or Brown-headed Cowbird (both rare in winter). A scope is recommended for this. Farther south is an obvious large pond surrounded by rushes. This can be surprisingly devoid of waterfowl at many times of the year but often in spring and fall (especially if the water is low enough to expose some mud), large numbers of ducks can occur. There's a small turn-around at the end of this dyke from which you can scan the mouth of the Okanagan River where it meets Osoyoos Lake. Sometimes a sandbar on which gulls can be seen loafing is visible, with more uncommon possibilities being pelicans, terns, and migrating waders in spring and fall. Note that partway along this dyke is a drop-structure/footbridge that can allow pedestrian access to the woodland block along the southwest dyke.

It's usually worthwhile to drive south along Black Sage Rd. (turn right at the old Haynes barn), also known as Radio Tower Rd. Barn Owls have nested here in the past but have not used these structures in over a decade (though the occasional Great Horned Owl is sometimes spotted roosting here). As you head south along Black Sage/Radio Tower Rd., there are two sandy pull-outs on the right/west side. These are great spots from which to look and listen for Yellow-breasted Chat in the breeding season as well as other riparian species. The native grasslands of the Haynes Lease Eco Reserve come down to the road here, and so other birds to look out for include Lazuli Bunting, Lark Sparrow, Vesper Sparrow, and, in some years, Grasshopper Sparrow (more often heard than seen). The road then descends and skirts a grazing pasture before coming up to an expansive marshy area. In winter, check the large rose thicket for flocks of American Tree Sparrow, and listen in the marsh for Marsh Wren and—if you're lucky—Swamp Sparrow (October–March). The road then climbs another hill, crosses a cattle-guard, and bends to the left directly beside an osprey platform. Pull over here. You're now on the Oliver-Osoyoos Indian Reserve, but birders are generally permitted to park here and scan down to the north end of Osoyoos Lake.

This vantage point also allows for great views of the Road 22 area as a whole. From here you can scope a wide variety of water birds throughout the year on the lake, the river, and adjacent oxbows and ponds. Red-necked Grebes nest in the shallow bay directly below you, and in winter this can be a good place to spot Red-breasted Mergansers out on the lake (Osoyoos Lake is the best site for this species in BC away from the coast in winter). If a sandbar is exposed near the mouth of the river, you never know what tired migrant might be resting there. My favourite time to visit this site is on a spring morning when birds are on the move. This site offers a great opportunity to practise your ear-birding, as the local marsh and riparian breeders are joined by the songs of northbound warblers, vireos, flycatchers, and more. On some days it's even possible to hear Chukar and Canyon Wren calling from the cliffs up above the vineyards!

18

CATHEDRAL LAKES PROVINCIAL PARK, KEREMEOS

BC IS FAMOUS for its high mountains, and those peaks hold more than spectacular landscapes of rock and ice—they also have a very distinctive bird fauna. Birders come to BC from all over Canada, and indeed North America, to search for enigmatic species that can't be found in the people-filled valleys. Mountain peaks are, almost by definition, difficult to access. Trails to alpine areas often begin at low elevations, necessitating arduous hikes to the meadows and ridges above. A number of sites in BC combine great scenery, good birds, and relatively easy access. One of my favourites is Cathedral Provincial Park. Also known simply as Cathedral Lakes, this park is nestled in the northern tip of

The alpine meadows of Cathedral Lakes Provincial Park are a favoured foraging area for Dusky Grouse in summer. Listen for the display hoots of males in early summer, and for the warning clucks of females calling to their brood of chicks.

the Cascade Range, a high treeless ridge with cirques carved out of its northern flanks, each cirque holding an exquisite lake.

BIRDING GUIDE

You can't drive up to Cathedral Lakes, but you can pay for that service. Alternatively, if you have the energy and time, you can make the long trek on foot, making your discoveries on the mountaintops that much more enjoyable. Whether you hike or ride, the trail begins on the banks of the Ashnola River. The river runs clear and cold out of the mountains and is a good place to look for two special species that breed along its banks and forage for insect larvae and fish eggs under its well-worn stones: Harlequin Duck and American Dipper.

From the Ashnola River, Lakeview Trail climbs steeply, following the west side of Lakeview Creek to Quiniscoe Lake. If you're riding in the Cathedral Lakes Lodge four-wheel drive vehicle, you won't be doing any birding along this route, but if you're hiking you'll have plenty of time to stop, look, and listen for Douglas-fir forest birds such as Hammond's Flycatchers, Mountain Chickadees, and Western Tanagers. I must admit, I'd definitely recommend the vehicle ride—it comes at a price, but it gives you two more days on the mountaintops and there will be plenty of opportunity for exercise once you're up there!

The trail and jeep road end at Quiniscoe Lake. Like all the lakes in the park, Quiniscoe is a jewel set in an alpine cirque near treeline. However you got here, you'll probably want to relax a bit around Quiniscoe and take in the spectacular scenery, the fresh mountain air, and a few good birds. Clark's Nutcrackers are one of the common denizens of the lodge area; their raucous calls make them easy to find, and they can be quite tame in this spot. These relatives of crows and jays habitually store whitebark pine seeds in the late summer and fall as a winter food supply, but they also eat a wide variety of other food, and are not above snitching part of your lunch if you look the other way. The nutcracker's cousin, the Gray Jay (aka Whiskey Jack), is also common in the forests around the lodge.

There are a number of short walks from Quiniscoe Lake if you'd like to ease into the beautiful scenery—a hike around the lake itself or the short trail to Lake of the Woods (a fine place to camp if that's your plan) and Pyramid Lake are good options. These trails go through mature Engelmann spruce-subalpine fir forest, though most of the older spruce trees have been killed by spruce bark beetle in the past decade. American Three-toed Woodpeckers have been abundant as a result, but this status may change as the beetle attack wanes. Spruce Grouse are relatively easy to find along any of the forested trails in the core area of the park; the larger, grayer Dusky Grouse (some may show intergradation with Sooty Grouse, the coastal Blue Grouse species) are usually found in the subalpine meadows on the ridges. The common forest birds include Pacific Wren, Mountain and Boreal Chickadees, Red-breasted Nuthatch, Ruby-crowned and Golden-crowned Kinglets, Hermit and Varied Thrushes, Townsend's and Yellow-rumped Warblers, and Pine Grosbeaks. If you venture out after dark on a summer evening, listen for the begging calls of young Boreal Owls!

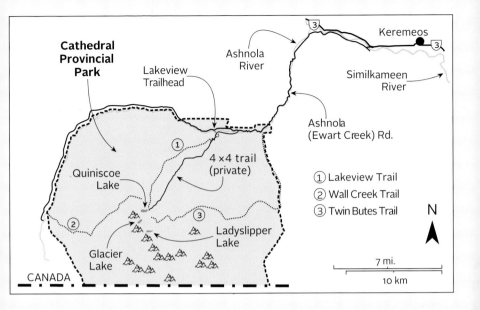

Cathedral Provincial Park

Lakeview Trailhead

Ashnola River

Keremeos

3

3

Similkameen River

Ashnola (Ewart Creek) Rd.

1

4 ×4 trail (private)

Quiniscoe Lake

3

① Lakeview Trail
② Wall Creek Trail
③ Twin Butes Trail

2

Ladyslipper Lake

Glacier Lake

CANADA

N

7 mi.

10 km

GETTING THERE

Take the Ashnola River Rd. (turn south off Hwy. 3, 4.8 km/3 mi. west of Keremeos) for 20.8 km (12.9 mi.) to the Cathedral Lakes Lodge base camp; the Lakeview Trail Head (for those hiking into the park) is about 2 km farther down the road. Contact Cathedral Lakes Lodge for information on transportation into the park or accommodation at the lodge (http://cathedrallakes.ca). If you wish to camp in the park, check www.env.gov.bc.ca/bcparks/explore/parkpgs/cathedral for information about fees and trails.

With just a little more effort you can hike to two exquisite lakes set in somewhat higher cirques: Glacier Lake and Ladyslipper Lake. In and around the alpine meadows around these lakes are found Horned Larks, American Pipits and Savannah Sparrows. Watch for Golden Eagles soaring over the ridges, and if you're lucky, a Prairie Falcon might rocket by. Barrow's Goldeneyes nest around the lakes, and you can often see a female leading a flotilla of tiny black-and-white ducklings on the azure water. Watch for Spotted Sandpipers teetering on the water's edge, and occasionally their Arctic-nesting relatives, Baird's Sandpipers, put in an appearance on their way to South America.

But the real reason to go to Cathedral Lakes is to explore the high rim trail that offers unparalleled vistas and superb alpine birding. It takes a bit of effort to climb to the 2,500 m (8,000 ft.) elevation ridge, but it's completely worth it. This is where you have a very good chance (but it always takes a bit of luck!) of finding a White-tailed Ptarmigan, that holy grail of high-alpine birding. The peak of Quiniscoe Mountain and the area around Stone City are the best spots in my experience. Watch for Gray-crowned Rosy Finches as well, especially around snowfields, where these birds feed on insects that have been grounded and refrigerated. On sunny days there are often a few Black Swifts twittering over the mountain peaks, catching the bugs that are still flying.

There are many other trails to explore around Cathedral Lakes—you should spend at least three days if you can, and longer if you'd like to really experience this extraordinary area. The best times to visit are from late June through early September, but if the weather is good and snowpacks are low, that season can extend from early June through early October. Mountain flower blooms usually peak in July, and the alpine larches turn the mountainsides golden in late September.

—19—

KOKANEE CREEK PROVINCIAL PARK, NELSON

W ITH SO MANY interesting nooks and crannies to explore in the West Kootenay Region, it's difficult to single out one or two spots for the purposes of this book. Kokanee Creek Park is a favourite site among local birders, as it combines productive year-round birding with the gorgeous scenery of Kootenay Lake and the Selkirk Mountains. The roughly two hundred species that have been recorded here are a testament to the diversity of habitats present as well as the dynamic changes that each season brings.

Most visitors from outside the Nelson area tend to pass through in summer when water bird numbers are down, but this is a great time to spot a variety of nesting songbirds,

In summer, the forests of the Kootenay region ring with birdsong. Identifying them as you lie in your tent can be a fun game, but of course seeing them—like this Yellow Warbler—is better still. LIRON GERTSMAN

and spring or late summer/early fall brings the chance of seeing a few shorebirds near the creek mouth, including local rarities such as Black-bellied Plover, American Avocet, and Wilson's Phalarope. August–September is the peak of the Kokanee salmon spawning season, and there are good viewing opportunities at a small spawning channel, with more information about the annual event at the visitor centre. The dying fish and new eggs also attract a number of birds, of course—mostly gulls, loons, and grebes, but also some local Mallards that have learned to feed on Kokanee eggs by stirring up the substrate with their feet in the shallow spawning channel. They also gorge themselves on the decaying carcasses, proving that ducks will eat more than just grass, seeds, and bread!

Kokanee Creek Provincial Park is also one of the most popular camping areas in the region (most sites are open May 1–September 30), with a great beach for swimming in summer. Outside of camping season, the day-use area is open year-round and birders can always find some quiet corners of the park to explore.

The park gained more widespread fame among birders in December 2014 when the province's first White-eyed Vireo was discovered foraging in some thick brush. Unfortunately, it only stuck around for about a week, but it shows that the potential for oddball birds remains, no matter the season— in July 2007 a Brown Pelican showed up at the park, the first Interior record of the species in Canada!

BIRDING GUIDE

In spring and summer the park is good for songbirds, especially riparian species such as Willow Flycatcher, Red-eyed

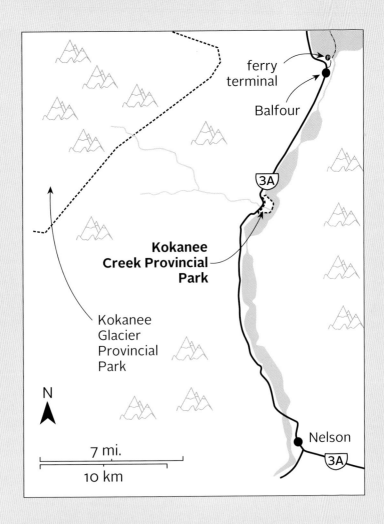

GETTING THERE

From downtown Nelson, drive north across the bridge over the narrow arm of Kootenay Lake (north end of Nelson Ave.), then continue northeast along Hwy. 3A for about 20 km (12.4 mi.) until you reach the park. From Balfour (ferry to Crawford Bay), it's around 12 km (7.5 mi.) west toward Nelson. From Hwy. 6 (Castlegar or Salmo), follow signs for Hwy. 3A East, then once across the bridge follow the instructions above.

Vireo, and Gray Catbird. Wood Ducks can be found in the beaver ponds on the west side of the creek while Belted Kingfishers often nest in the eroding bank at the mouth of the creek. Other local breeders of note include an American Dipper pair that consistently nests under the highway bridge within the park, often raising two broods each season. Merlins and Osprey both nest in the vicinity of the park and Barred Owls have also raised young not far from the visitor centre. The mature conifer forest near the visitor centre and across the footbridge at the group camping area is a reliable area for both Chestnut-backed Chickadee and Townsend's Warbler.

Migration season brings intriguing mixes of birds through the park. Mountain Bluebirds often show up in spring, with fall being the best time for sparrows. White-crowned, Lincoln's, and Savannah are the most common species encountered at this time, but rarer species like Golden-crowned, White-throated, Harris's, and Swamp have also been recorded. From August into early November gulls gather at the creek mouth to take advantage of the Kokanee spawning run. Ring-billed, California, and Herring are the common species, but a few Bonaparte's can show up as well.

Ospreys leave in the fall and are replaced by good numbers of Bald Eagles that remain all winter, hunting the American Coots and Horned Grebes that gather on the lake. Northern Pygmy-Owls are also around in the colder months, keeping an eye out for potential prey, including Bohemian Waxwing, Pine Grosbeak, and Common Redpoll.

Normally a skulking marsh species, the Sora will often venture out into the open when water levels drop in late summer. Watch for them wading along the muddy fringes of cattail clumps at the south end of Duck Lake. ILYA POVALYAEV

20

DUCK LAKE, CRESTON

T'S NO SECRET that wetland habitats have suffered tremendously across the province, and indeed the globe, due to a number of factors including agricultural development and increased toxins and sedimentation in our watercourses. However, the Creston Valley Wildlife Management Area is a shining example of what can happen when humans work responsibly to safeguard these wetlands and help them to flourish. Covering 6,900 hectares (17,050 acres) of Crown land, it was classified as a "wetland of international importance" in 1994, owing to its numerous ecological values, including being the only provincial breeding site of Forster's Terns, hosting one of only two Western Grebe nesting colonies, and being one of the few reliable sites to find Leopard

Frogs and Coeur d'Alene Salamanders in BC. Visitors to the area are struck by the expansiveness of the wetlands and the abundance of birdlife in the area, including some of the densest breeding populations of Wood Duck, American Bittern (though sadly they seem to be declining in numbers in recent years), American Coot, Yellow Warbler, and Lazuli Bunting. It's also a critical staging area for migrating waterfowl and a wonderful area for raptors in the winter.

I've chosen to cover only the northeastern section of the wetland complex (Duck Lake), as it generally offers the most diversity of birdlife on a year-round basis. Any visit to this area, however, should include a stop at the main CVWMA Visitor's Centre at Corn Creek Marsh. In summer, naturalists offer guided canoe tours of the marsh and can offer more information about recent sightings and access information for the rest of the reserve. This centre is well signed on the south side of Hwy. 3 west of Creston (west side of the valley).

BIRDING GUIDE

Between spring and fall, the slough you pass before turning right/north onto Channel Rd. is often filled with Wood Ducks, sometimes hundreds. Many other ducks frequent this remnant course of the Old Goat River—the abundance and variety will depend on the time of year. From the start of Channel Rd., it's just under 6 km (3.7 mi.) to Duck Lake. Along the way you may hear the perpetual summer song of Red-eyed Vireos somewhere high up in the cottonwoods, along with the chatter of Bullock's Orioles, the emphatic *chebek! chebek!* of a feisty Least Flycatcher and the plaintive *peeeer* of the Western Wood-Pewee. In winter, keep an eye open for Northern Shrikes scanning the horizon from

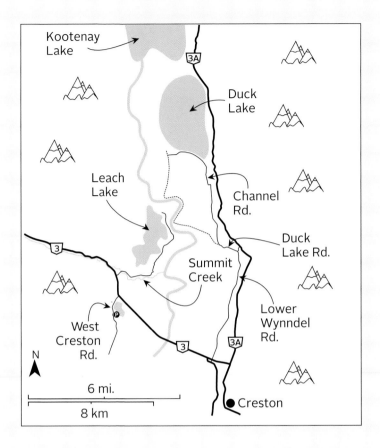

Kootenay Lake

3A

Duck Lake

Leach Lake

Channel Rd.

Duck Lake Rd.

Summit Creek

Lower Wynndel Rd.

3

3

3A

West Creston Rd.

P

N

6 mi.

8 km

Creston

GETTING THERE

To reach the Valley's most popular birding area, exit off Hwy. 3 south onto Hwy. 21 (signed for the US border though you won't be heading in that direction), then make an immediate left to go through the tunnel northward onto Lower Wynndel Rd. Drive 6.8 km (4 mi.) north then turn left (west) onto Duck Lake Rd.— slow down, be ready for the turn, and be alert for oncoming vehicles as this is a bit of an awkward intersection. From Hwy. 3A (driving between Creston and Kootenay Lake) you can turn west onto the other end of Lower Wynndel Rd.; Duck Lake Rd. will come up quickly on the right. Once on Duck Lake Rd., drive for just over 1 km (0.6 mi.) then make a right onto Channel Rd. after crossing a big slough. Continue north to reach the south end of Duck Lake.

prominent perches on the left/west side of the road, and in April–June, check any shrike carefully as the rare Loggerhead Shrike has turned up multiple times here. In early spring and late fall you may be lucky enough to spot a flock of migrating Sandhill Cranes resting or feeding out in the fields.

As the road meets the south end of Duck Lake, it merges onto a dyke where there are several pull-offs to bird the lake and marshes on either side. There should be lots to look at no matter what time of year you visit, but March–April is best for the waterfowl migration spectacle. While they're still relatively rare in other Interior valleys, Greater White-fronted Geese pass through in groups of hundreds or even thousands in spring, and both species of swans also stop over in the fields and on the lake in impressive groupings.

During the breeding season, scan through the large summer flotilla of Western Grebes for any stray Clark's Grebes—though this can be a difficult task if the birds are far out. If there's any exposed mud between mid-April and May, good numbers of shorebirds can be seen.

Between spring and early fall, look for Forster's Terns on either side of the dyke. This is the only known breeding area in the province, but the terns aren't always consistent in where they nest as water levels vary each year. Sometimes adults can be seen feeding young at this location; in other years they will be more numerous around Leach Lake or Six Mile Slough. If you arrive late in the summer after the young have fledged and cannot see any nearby, try scanning out along the far edges of Duck Lake, as they move around quite a bit. They'll also move over to the south end of Kootenay Lake at times.

As with Leach Lake and Corn Creek Marsh, birders can expect a bounty of marsh-loving species in this area from the secretive Marsh Wren and American Bittern to the noisy blackbird sentinels. Scan the tall trees to the west and southwest of Duck Lake to see the nesting colony of Double-crested Cormorants. The willows along the dyke are well known for their rarities potential, so be vigilant and check through any mixed migrant flocks that might be passing. Among the long list of rarities, this patch has turned up multiple Sage Thrashers and Loggerhead Shrikes. In winter, the willows and reed-beds on either side are a favourite haunt of a small flock of American Tree Sparrows.

Road conditions can be quite muddy or snowy depending on the time of year, so be careful when driving a small car. At the west end of the dyke (along the south side of Duck Lake) you'll hit a T-junction. Turning right will take you north along the west side of the lake, through nice riparian habitat before dead-ending in just over 6 km (3.7 mi.). It's usually possible to complete a loop by turning left at this junction, which will soon lead you to the western end of Duck Lake Rd. (which leads east back to the Channel Rd. junction).

The Eastern Kingbird is a vigorous defender of its territory, and in summer pairs can often be seen chasing ravens and raptors that have ventured too close to their nest. JOSHUA BROWN

21

COLUMBIA RIVER WETLANDS, ROCKY MOUNTAINS

ERHAPS THE MOST striking geographical feature of eastern BC is the fault line along the Rocky Mountains' western flank, extending 1,600 km (around 1,000 mi.) from Flathead Lake in Montana all the way up to the Yukon border. Commonly known as the Rocky Mountain Trench (and also as The Valley of a Thousand Peaks), it drains four major river basins, of which the Liard and Peace flow eventually into the Arctic Ocean, and the Fraser and Columbia into the Pacific. It's a natural corridor for avian migration, and narrow sections of the valley known as bottlenecks can be great places to seek out high numbers of birds, including rarities, forced down by inclement weather in spring and fall. Evidence of this can be clearly demonstrated by the data from the Mackenzie Nature Observatory on Williston Lake, extensive anecdotal observations from the McBride and Valemount areas, and the efforts of one dedicated birder in the Blaeberry (near Golden), who has documented no fewer than 215 species in the vicinity of his property, including many interesting vagrants such as Broad-tailed Hummingbird, Purple Martin, Philadelphia Vireo, Great Crested Flycatcher, and (eastern) Winter Wren.

The southern portion of the Trench, from Golden to the US border, is no exception to this trend, and there have been many interesting records, including an increasing number of White-faced Ibis in recent years. Adding to its topographical strategic value, the valley bottom here is characterized by some of the most extensive and pristine wetland and riparian habitats left in the province.

The diversity of birds during the summer months is due to the great variety of habitats found along the southern Rocky Mountain Trench and its two main rivers: the Columbia and Kootenay. The fascinating journey to the sea of these two major watercourses is directly tied in with the unique geography of the region and the ecosystems that have resulted from it. The Kootenay River comes out of the Rockies just south of Columbia Lake at Canal Flats. Here, at the headwaters of the mighty Columbia, the rivers are close to touching but instead, the Kootenay River flows south into Montana before swinging west into Idaho, then north through the Creston Valley, and past Kokanee Creek and Nelson before finally joining the now massive Columbia River at Castlegar. Along the way it passes through wet

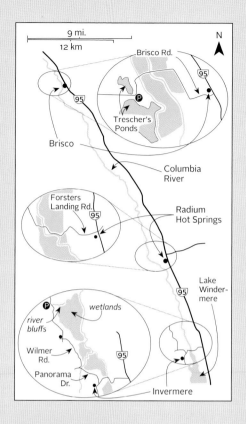

GETTING THERE

The picturesque town of Invermere, at the north end of Lake Windermere, is a 1.5 hour drive north from Cranbrook along Hwy. 93 or about 1.25 hours south of Golden. The areas described above provide ample distractions for anyone travelling from coastal BC to the Rocky Mountains.

and dry valleys, narrow canyons, and flat agricultural areas. The Columbia starts by flowing north out of Columbia Lake, through the towns of Invermere and Golden, then, swinging around through the Kinbasket Reservoir, it turns south and passes Revelstoke and Nakusp, before meeting the

Kootenay, then cutting through the middle of Washington State, turning west along the Oregon border, and reaching the sea at Astoria. With no fewer than fourteen hydroelectric dams along its route, plus important cities such as Portland, Oregon, and extensive agricultural areas, the Columbia is undoubtedly one of the most important rivers to humans in North America.

From a birding standpoint, the Columbia's initial south-to-north route gives it the peculiar feature of beginning in a warm, dry valley of Ponderosa Pines and scattered sagebrush where Long-billed Curlews, Lewis's Woodpeckers, and Pygmy Nuthatches can be found, before flowing downhill through cool boreal forests of fir and spruce where moose, wolves, and nesting birds like Spruce Grouse, American Three-toed Woodpecker, and Boreal Chickadee can be seen near the water's edge!

This area is far too large to include in one chapter, therefore I will briefly focus on one of my favourite sections of the Rocky Mountain Trench: the Columbia River Wetlands from Invermere north to Brisco. This area boasts both stunning scenery and great birding. If you're travelling in May, I would highly recommend taking part in the annual Wings Over the Rockies birding festival (wingsovertherockies.org). It's based in Invermere but includes guided nature tours throughout the southern Rocky Mountain Trench during a fabulous time of year.

BIRDING GUIDE

Some of the best of these Columbia River wetlands are protected in the Wilmer National Wildlife Area. Turn west off Hwy. 93/95 and proceed down the hill and into the town of

Invermere. Cross the railway tracks, turn north onto Panorama Dr., and follow it across the Toby Creek Bridge. Take the first right/north onto Wilmer Rd. Proceed into the village of Wilmer, turning right onto Main Ave., which soon leaves town and becomes Westside Rd. After about 2 km (1.2 mi.) on Westside Rd., you'll see a pull-off on the right/east side of the road and National Wildlife Area signs. Park up and follow the trail along the grassy slopes above spectacular silt bluffs. Grassland species such as American Kestrel and Vesper Sparrows are common here, and the views of the wetlands are exceptional (a spotting scope is recommended).

For some more great spots farther north, return to Hwy. 93/95 then turn north toward Radium Hot Springs. At the four-way stop in Radium, turn left onto Forster's Landing Rd. At the bottom of the hill, this road skirts the south side of the Radium mill ponds, a great site for waterfowl, Yellow-headed Blackbirds, and Bullock's Orioles. It's very productive during spring and fall migration, but even in mid-summer good birds such as Wood Duck and Hooded Merganser can be found. Return to the highway, drive about 30 km (about 19 mi.) north from Radium to the village of Brisco, and turn left onto Brisco Rd. The road turns north/right at a mill, then swings west/left to cross the wetlands. After crossing the river, the road turns sharply south/left, then sharply west/right. Immediately after this last corner, you'll see two marshy ponds on either side of the road. These ponds, known locally as Trescher's Ponds, are good for species such as Sora, Virginia Rail, and Marsh Wren; check the hayfields on the south side of the road for Bobolinks.

The name "Magnolia Warbler" is quite misleading during the breeding season. Around Mount Robson, they are most often associated with spruce trees in the valley bottom. LIRON GERTSMAN

22

MOUNT ROBSON, ROCKY MOUNTAINS

IRDING IS OFTEN most exciting along biophysical boundaries, places where you cross from forest to grassland or mountains to plains on a grand scale. One of the most obvious of these natural borders is the Rocky Mountains, the spine of the continent. Many western species reach their easternmost extent along this spectacular mountain range, and many eastern species go no farther west. For a birder used to the species found in the valleys of BC, the Rockies combine magnificent scenery with the added possibility of species not usually seen at home. And perhaps the best site for this thrilling mix is Mount Robson.

From the west, take Hwy. 16 or 5. The two highways meet at Tête Jaune Cache (the yellow-headed fur trader who gave the highway its name, and referred to locally as "TEE-zhawn"). After the junction, the road swings eastward, following the Fraser River valley into the heart of the Rockies. The mountains flanking the highway are spectacular, but don't really prepare you for the sight that you encounter around a corner a few kilometres east—the face of Mount Robson, the highest peak in the Canadian Rockies, a vertical wall of rock 3 km high (over 9,000 feet). This view is reason enough to visit Mount Robson; the diverse bird fauna makes the trip even more worthwhile.

Like many mountain sites in BC, Mount Robson Provincial Park has a remarkable diversity of habitats—from the cedar-hemlock rainforests along the Fraser River in the west end of the park to the extensive marshes at Moose Lake, the spruce-fir forests on the mountainsides and the alpine meadows at higher elevations. These diverse habitats naturally result in a wide variety of bird species. Some species are common throughout the valley forests, particularly those typical of the mountains of western North America, such as Hammond's Flycatcher, Steller's Jay, and Townsend's Warbler.

BIRDING GUIDE

Probably the best way to start a birding visit to Mount Robson is to make the easy hike to Kinney Lake. The road to the trailhead leaves from the park visitor centre on the north side of the highway. You can make an immediate detour to Robson River campground—a stroll along the river through stunted spruce could net you a singing Blackpoll Warbler, if your ears are young enough to hear the extraordinarily

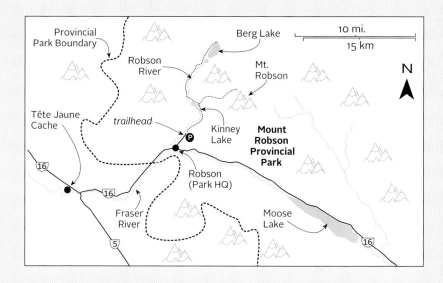

GETTING THERE

Mount Robson is hard to miss. You can drive to it via the Yellowhead Hwy. (16) from Prince George in the west (about 3 hours), from the south up the North Thompson Valley (Hwy. 5) from Kamloops (3 hours 45 minutes), or from Edmonton, AB, in the east (just under 5 hours).

high-pitched song. Frequent stops along the trailhead road are usually very productive and the road makes a great walking route for early morning birding. In late May and June, the forests ring with warbler song, including more eastern specialty species such as Magnolia and Tennessee. The insistent, repetitive *chebek!* songs of Least Flycatchers often add to that eastern flavour. A wooded wetland along the road often has a variety of ducks, including Ring-necked Duck, while Northern Waterthrush and Lincoln's Sparrows sing loudly from the shrubs at the water's edge.

The hike to Kinney Lake and Berg Lake follows the course of the Robson River as it tumbles through one of the most spectacular valleys on earth, and birding usually takes a back seat to the scenery. The trail is relatively flat as far as Kinney Lake, then climbs steeply through the Valley of a Thousand Falls to Berg Lake. The high forests at Berg Lake are home to Boreal Chickadees; watch for Harlequin Ducks on the lake itself. Beyond Berg Lake, the river winds through gravel flats below Robson Glacier; listen for the mournful whistles of Golden-crowned Sparrows as they sing "Oh poor me."

Moose Lake lies along the highway in the centre of Mount Robson Provincial Park. It's one of the few large lakes at a moderate elevation in the Canadian Rockies and can have some surprising birds, especially during migration periods when its waters offer a resting place for ducks, loons, and grebes. In May and early June you might encounter ocean-going ducks such as Surf Scoter, White-winged Scoter, and Long-tailed Duck resting on the water on their way to breeding grounds farther north and east. Common Mergansers and Common Loons can be seen all summer long. East of Moose Lake is a large marsh of sedges, willows, and alders formed along the meandering channel of the Fraser River. This marsh marks a particular avian boundary: where Willow Flycatchers and Alder Flycatchers meet. These two species were formerly considered a single species, the Traill's Flycatcher, but research on the Cariboo Plateau between Williams Lake and Lac La Hache showed that there were two species—one that sang FITZ-bew! (Willow) and another that sang fee-BEE-o! (Alder). Another interesting denizen of the Moose Lake marshes is the Rusty Blackbird, a characteristic species of the boreal forest that has suffered a dramatic decline of 85–98% in its population over the past forty years. The causes of this collapse are not well understood but likely relate to a combination of pressure from the oil, gas, mining, and forestry industries on their boreal nesting grounds, and poisoning of blackbird flocks by farmers in the southeastern USA where most of the population overwinters in large mixed flocks.

Look over the marsh itself for water birds such as Ring-necked Ducks, Blue-winged and Cinnamon Teals, and Red-necked Grebes, and listen for the winnowing of Wilson's Snipes overhead. Northern Waterthrush and Common Yellowthroat are common songbirds around the edges of the wetlands.

From Moose Lake the highway provides access to broad areas of subalpine forest. At sites such as Lucerne Campground, watch for Spruce Grouse, American Three-toed Woodpecker, and Pine Grosbeak. In some years, the valley is invaded by large numbers of White-winged Crossbills, a species that roams the boreal forests around the Northern Hemisphere, searching for good spruce cone crops. They often arrive in mid-summer when other species have fallen silent, and their loud, long, canary-like songs dominate the soundscape of the Rockies.

Ospreys have made a significant recovery since the DDT era and are now a common sight throughout the interior of British Columbia including Scout Island in Williams Lake. LIRON GERTSMAN

23

SCOUT ISLAND, WILLIAMS LAKE

SCOUT ISLAND IS a relatively small chunk of land at the west end of Williams Lake in the Cariboo. Dotted with thick willows and shrubs, and surrounded by cattail marshes, it hosts an abundance of birdlife from spring through fall and is accessible via a causeway road just before the city of Williams Lake (if driving from the south along Hwy. 97). There are plenty of similar locations throughout the province, but the added value of Scout Island is its wonderful convenience for those travelling along the major highway of central BC. In other words, it's one of the best birding "rest stops" one could hope for, equipped with toilets and picnicking facilities, as well as a nature house with knowledgeable naturalists who can inform you about recent sightings.

With close to 200 species recorded at this relatively small site, it's clear that there's plenty on offer, from the abundant nesting waterfowl and marsh birds to the denizens of riparian thickets such as Veery, Gray Catbird, and Bullock's Oriole (all nearing the northern limits of their breeding ranges, though all have been expanding gradually in recent years). In summer, there are almost always a few American White Pelicans loafing about in the northwest marsh, and rare species such as Great Egret, Green Heron, and Harris's Sparrow have turned up in the past. It's well situated along a migration corridor, so expect mixed flocks of warblers and sparrows in April/May and August/September, including Tennessee and Blackpoll Warblers that appear to be rare but regular in late summer. Williams Lake itself is a great place for waterfowl, particularly in early spring and late fall but also throughout the summer with so many nesting species present. The lake is frozen for much of the winter and this is a decidedly quiet time on the island.

BIRDING GUIDE

Start by checking in at the nature house/visitor centre to see if any guided walks are being offered or if they have any tips about recent sightings. The trees and shrubs right around the building can be great for warblers, vireos, and flycatchers in migration. From the parking area/nature house there are loop trails to the west (in the direction of town) or east out toward the lake. Walking west will take you past some thick shrubs as well as open grassland areas—the latter being great for sparrows on migration. This area will give you access to some of the nicer marshes around Scout

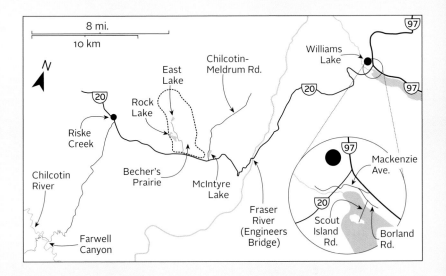

GETTING THERE

Turn south off Hwy. 97 onto Hwy. 20, then make an immediate left onto Mackenzie Ave. before turning right on Borland and right again onto Scout Island Rd. The centre is only about 1 km (0.6 mi.) by road from Hwy. 20. From the Tim Hortons on the highway you can scan the marshes and lake from the parking lot. The access will be obvious.

Island. Walking east will ultimately lead you onto a narrow peninsula jutting out into Williams Lake. This area can be good for mixed migrant flocks in spring, late summer, and fall, and it's a great place to scope the lake and surrounding marshes.

Most grassland birds are brown and streaky so clearly the Mountain Bluebird didn't get the memo! These birds have benefited from hundreds of nest-boxes put up along fencelines by dedicated volunteers. LIRON GERTSMAN

24

BECHER'S PRAIRIE, CHILCOTIN PLATEAU

THERE ARE PLACES in BC that are hidden gems—strikingly beautiful in a province full of spectacular scenery, diverse in natural history, and relatively easy to get to, but largely unknown. Becher's Prairie is not only all of these things, but also simply surprising. Most visitors—and many residents—think of BC as a world of high mountains, roaring rivers, and endless forests, so the word "prairie" seems out of place from the start.

At the southwestern tip of the vast Chilcotin Plateau is a small sea of grass, studded with lakes and ponds, aspen copses, and fingers of pine forest. Becher's Prairie is a small prairie set in the midst of mountains and forests, looking more like a part of Alberta or Saskatchewan than BC. On the north and west it's bounded by extensive forests; on the south and east, the prairie plunges over basalt cliffs and silt bluffs to the Chilcotin and Fraser Rivers. Its habitats are a glorious mix of conifer forest, prairie potholes, and semi-desert grasslands.

I worked on Becher's Prairie with my two brothers for six months in 1978, studying aquatic insects in the diverse lakes and ponds scattered across the grasslands. We lived in a forestry camp in Riske Creek, a tiny community on the western edge of the prairie, and spent our days driving the dirt tracks that wandered across the landscape, skirting around clumps of forest and fording small streams. It was a totally new landscape with wildlife spectacles I hadn't imagined possible in BC: lakes covered in so many ducks and grebes that it took us a half hour to count them all; coveys of Sharp-tailed Grouse exploding out of the grass, seeking cover in clumps of snowberry and aspen; and flocks of Lapland Longspurs migrating south against an azure September sky.

This was truly the edge of the Wild West, the gravel road extending past Riske Creek for hundreds of kilometres through ranchland and forest, the road signs full of history and mystery—Alexis Creek, Puntzi, Tatlayoko Lake, Kleena Kleene, Anahim. We stopped in at the café at Hanceville, the next community west from Riske Creek, and after settling down with our coffees I realized that everyone else in the place was speaking Tsilhqot'in. That coffee stop immediately changed my perception of the depth and importance of Native cultures in BC. And in the fall, the local cowboys appeared, driving cattle herds and separating out those with their brands, cutting the cattle along the shoreline of Rock Lake.

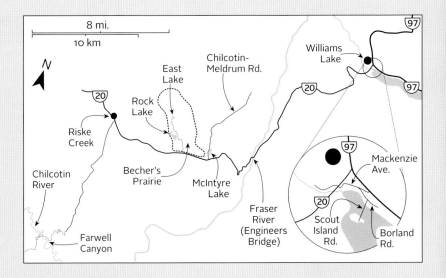

GETTING THERE

To reach the Prairie, head for Williams Lake on Hwy. 97, then turn west onto Hwy. 20, following signs for City Centre; once across town continue on Hwy. 20 (Chilcotin-Bella Coola). (See above for detailed directions.)

BIRDING GUIDE

It's easier to get to Becher's Prairie now than it was back in the 1970s, but in many ways little has changed. Turn west at Williams Lake, off Hwy. 97 and onto Hwy. 20, also known as the Chilcotin Hwy. (but officially called the Alexander Mackenzie Hwy.). The trip to Becher's Prairie from Williams Lake is relatively short. It begins with a descent off the Cariboo Plateau and into the deep valley of the Fraser River, which you cross on the Engineers Bridge. It's often worth a stop just past the bridge to enjoy the spectacular scenery

Rock Lake could easily be a mistaken for one of the hundreds of prairie potholes that dot southern Saskatchewan. RICHARD CANNINGS

and look and listen for some of the dry grassland special-ties you probably won't see up on the plateau—especially the lovely Lazuli Bunting. The highway then climbs onto the Chilcotin Plateau, offering good views of the columnar basalt bluffs that mark the edge of the geological skin of the plateau. You suddenly pop out of the Fraser River valley and find yourself on the gently rolling topography of the plateau. About 1 km (0.6 mi.) to the west you pass the Chilcotin-Meldrum Rd. on the north side of the highway. There's a Forest Service campsite at McIntyre Lake, only a few hun-dred metres/yards off the highway.

About 3.5 km (2.2 mi.) west of the Chilcotin-Meldrum Rd. junction, a small track goes north off the highway. This is the road to Rock Lake and other sites in the heart of Becher's Prairie, and should be your first destination when exploring the area. Watch and listen for breeding Greater Yellowlegs in the marshy pond west of the track about 1 km (0.6 mi.) in. While most birders are familiar with this species in migration, relatively few see it on its breeding grounds across the mid-latitudes of Canada. The species' territorial song, a rollicking alREDDy- alREDDy- alREDDy! can be heard on spring mornings.

The track winds for another 1 km (0.6 mi.) between copses of trees (listen for Red-naped Sapsuckers drumming and Least Flycatchers singing from the aspens) before reaching Rock Lake, its southern shore cloaked in forest and its northern shore open grass. Farther along the lake you'll see the rocky hillock on the north side of the road that gives the lake its name; this feature is famous as a significant hibernaculum for garter snakes. In spring or fall you may be lucky enough to see hundreds of snakes sunning themselves on the rocks, but if you want to see birds, just scan the lake (outside of winter). It's usually covered with a large variety of ducks—Gadwall, American Wigeon, Mallard, Blue-winged, Cinnamon and Green-winged Teal, Northern Shoveler, Redhead, Ring-necked Duck, Lesser Scaup, Bufflehead, Barrow's Goldeneye, and Ruddy Duck are all common breeding species here. During migration periods, watch for less common waterfowl such as Surf and White-winged Scoters and Long-tailed Duck, and Bonaparte's Gulls and shorebirds such as Solitary, Stilt, Baird's, Least, Semipalmated, and Pectoral Sandpipers.

One of the big attractions of Rock Lake is the large colony of Eared Grebes tucked into the bulrushes at the western end of the lake. The numbers vary every year, but usually there are around a hundred or more pairs of these elegant birds nesting here. Also in the marsh are good numbers of nesting Marsh Wrens and Yellow-headed Blackbirds. If you listen to the dawn chorus coming from the forest on the far side of the lake, you might pick out the distinctive quick-THREE-beers! of an Olive-sided Flycatcher or the delicate songs of Swainson's and Hermit Thrushes. The open grasslands are home to Horned Larks, Vesper Sparrows, and Western Meadowlarks.

The next large lake along the road is East Lake, also usually covered with waterfowl and well worth a lengthy stop. Beyond this point the track enters a large military training area; usually access to the area is restricted, so don't enter without inquiring locally. There's an unmarked track to the southwest that would take you to Riske Creek, but it's probably best to turn around here and return to the highway.

Once on the highway, drive about 10 km (6.2 mi.) west to the hamlet of Riske Creek. Just east of the well-signed Chilcotin Lodge is the Farwell Canyon Rd. leading south off the highway (if you reach Stack Valley Rd. and the hotel, Farwell Canyon Rd. is about 500 m/yd. back toward Williams Lake). This is well worth a day trip for its combination of spectacular scenery and birds. It's a good gravel road, but tends to be a bit dusty in late summer and is used by logging trucks coming out of the southern Chilcotin pine forests, so drive carefully and give every truck a wide berth.

The road winds through grassy hillsides mixed with patches of forests and aspen copses. Keep your eyes peeled for Sharp-tailed Grouse—a tough bird to find in BC but a regular resident of the Chilcotin grasslands. You pass a couple large alkaline ponds on the west side of the road; scan these in summer for breeding ducks such as Gadwall, American Wigeon, Green-winged Teal, and Canvasback. Wilson's Phalaropes also breed here, so watch for the big, colourful females as they court the duller males. In late July and August the salty shores of these ponds are good places to look for shorebirds such as Lesser Yellowlegs, Baird's Sandpiper, Sanderling, and Least Sandpiper.

After 15 km (9.3 mi.), you reach the deep valley of the Chilcotin River and the road begins to wind down the slopes in a series of tight switchbacks. At the top of the hill is a side road to the east with an information kiosk about the Junction Sheep Range Provincial Park, which protects land to the east of Farwell Canyon, where the Chilcotin River meets the Fraser River. If you have the time and a suitable vehicle (high clearance is recommended and four-wheel drive is necessary in wet conditions), take the small dirt road to the east and explore this gorgeous bit of country. Watch for Long-billed Curlews in the flatter grasslands, and Lewis's Woodpeckers in scattered big trees and snags. The park is named after the band of Bighorn Sheep that live on the steep slopes above the rivers.

If you continue down the Farwell Canyon Rd. to the Chilcotin River bridge, pause to take in the dramatic scenery of hoodoo cliffs above the river. In the late summer, salmon swim through the narrow canyon on their way to spawning grounds near Chilko Lake. Listen for singing Lazuli Buntings in the shrubs along the river and the loud chatter of White-throated Swifts overhead—this is one of the northernmost nesting sites in the world for this fast-flying species. For map, see page 159.

Rock Sandpipers are tough to find these days due to significant population declines and their penchant for sticking to remote rocky islets when migrating along BC's coast. LIRON GERTSMAN

25

SANDSPIT AIRPORT, HAIDA GWAII

IN BC, THERE are few regions better for finding rare birds than Haida Gwaii. Also known as the Queen Charlotte Islands, this archipelago sits across the wide but shallow Hecate Strait from Prince Rupert and within sight of the Alaska Panhandle. The North Pacific is a stormy place, and with so many birds from strong-flying geese to tiny hummingbirds making return trips to northern Canada, Alaska, and eastern Russia each year, it's no wonder that bad weather can push birds out to sea and down for emergency landings. Haida Gwaii acts as a haven for birds lost at sea. Imagine a tired songbird blown off-course from Russia or Alaska, struggling to stay airborne, and then suddenly catching sight of land. On the mainland there might be plenty of places for it to land, but on an island, its choices are limited. Much of Haida Gwaii is cloaked in thick coniferous forest, and therefore a bird such as a pipit or sparrow that favours grassy open areas is limited further. This is why airports and playing fields are often the most productive places to bird in the remote communities of coastal BC, and it's precisely why the community and adjacent airport of Sandspit (on Haida Gwaii's Moresby Island) is one of the best places to bird in the province. As the name suggests, the village and adjacent airport of Sandspit are located on a sandy peninsula that juts out into the Hecate Strait. This makes it very visible to passing birds and a convenient place for birders to visit and explore. Birding highlights over the years include Baikal Teal, Lesser Black-backed Gull, Least Tern, Eurasian Dotterel, Common Greenshank, Ruff, Red-necked Stint, Little Stint, Sky Lark, Eastern Yellow Wagtail, Red-throated Pipit, and Smith's Longspur.

BIRDING GUIDE

The birding guide here is fairly simple: Drive to the end of Beach Rd. (the main road that hugs the shoreline as you approach Sandspit from the west) and park at the southwest corner of the airport. From here, walk or bike around the perimeter of the airport—or return from whence you came.

Because of the airport's geography, it's a fantastic place for birding in general, from the large flocks of sea ducks and alcids offshore to the geese, raptors, and ground-foraging passerines that prefer the grassy areas around the runway. When big winds blow in off the Hecate Strait, shearwaters and fulmars can often be seen flying close to shore. Although many of these birds are around the airport at any

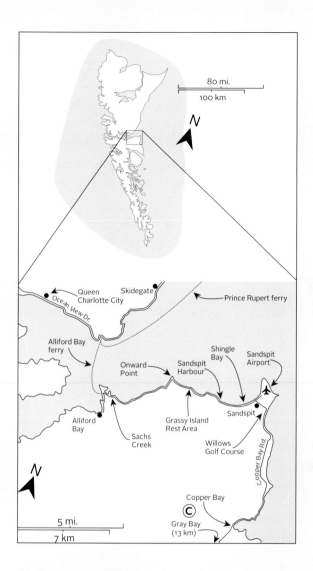

GETTING THERE

Sandspit Airport is, of course, an airport, so logically you can get to it using a plane (there are regular flights from Vancouver, Victoria, and Prince Rupert). Alternatively, you can take the car-ferry from Prince Rupert to Skidegate then cross over to Moresby Island on the Alliford Bay ferry before driving east to Sandspit.

time, if you're hoping to maximize your shorebirding experience, it's best to start the loop at least 1.5–2 hours before high tide. Shorebird flocks tend to concentrate around the Little Spit (northeast corner), so you should aim to be there at least 30 minutes before high tide. You may still run into feeding flocks along the western side of the peninsula or near the Big Spit at the northwest end. If the tide is low, the best area to search is probably out on the shingle flats just west of Little Spit or on the spit itself. Don't walk out on Big Spit—the tide can rise quickly and trap you. Once the tide has risen all the way, some shorebirds may continue to feed in the kelp racks along the shore, particularly near the base of Little Spit or along the east beach to the south. Otherwise, some of the flocks will sometimes fly onto the grassy fields along the runway, so scan carefully.

In addition to the shorebirds and seabirds, check the rose thickets and other shrubs for migrating sparrows and warblers. It's always worthwhile to scan migrating flocks of pipits or longspurs, as you never know what vagrant might be tagging along. In spring and fall, Short-eared Owls are often seen hunting around the perimeter of the airport, and Peregrine Falcons are usually one of the most prevalent raptors in the area.

When you reach the southeast corner of the airport, your progress might be blocked by a creek (depending on the time of year). There should be a small trail that skirts the water on the right/west side; this will take you out to the east end of School Rd., which you can use to walk back to your car. This entire loop is around 6 km (3.7 mi.) but it's only 3.5 km (2.2 mi.) if you arrange to get dropped off at one end and picked up at the other.

26

TUMBLER RIDGE

(Contributed in part by Charles Helm)

T UMBLER RIDGE REMAINS BC's youngest community. It was created in the wilderness of the eastern foothills of the Rockies in the early 1980s as the centre for the area's abundant metallurgical coal resources. Coal prices have subsequently fluctuated wildly, and mines have come and gone in typical boom and bust cycles. An unparalleled example of volunteer effort to diversify the economy and recognize the unique attributes of the community and its surrounding area has not only helped it survive, but has also propelled it into the international spotlight.

One of the catalysts for this was the discovery of dinosaur tracks by two young boys in a creek-bed just below town in 2000, when the extinction of the community due to mine closures was being predicted. This led to the formation of

The high-pitched staccato trill of the Blackpoll Warbler can be hard to hear for some. Spruce trees next to wetlands appear to be their favoured breeding habitat in Tumbler Ridge, and so Bullmoose Marshes is a reliable site in summer.
LIAM SINGH

the Tumbler Ridge Museum Foundation, the Dinosaur Discovery Gallery in town, and the adjoining Peace Region Palaeontology Research Centre. Tumbler Ridge is now the centre of excellence in vertebrate palaeontology (including paleo-ornithology) in the province, and a seemingly never-ending series of exquisite fossil discoveries has made international news.

This has been complemented by the development and maintenance by volunteers of the Wolverine Nordic and Mountain Society of almost 100 km (62 mi.) of hiking trails to areas of outstanding natural beauty and geological significance (including many fine birding localities). Together, the museum and the trails led to the volunteer-driven push for the coveted UNESCO Global Geopark status, which was conferred in September 2014. The Tumbler Ridge Global Geopark joins 110 others worldwide, and is only the second in North America and the first in the west. The Global Geopark status has the potential to further positively transform the nature of the community and the Peace Region.

The distribution of birds has everything to do with geology, geography, and relatively recent Pleistocene history, and is therefore part of the Geopark story. Tumbler Ridge is one of those precious localities in BC where "East meets West," exemplified by the story of the splitting of the Winter Wren into two species, the Pacific Wren and the Winter Wren. The research was conducted by scientists from UBC at the Quality Falls trail just northeast of town. Singing birds of both populations beside the trail were mist-netted and their blood subjected to mitochondrial DNA analysis, which clinched the evidence in support of the split. This saga is interpreted through an exhibit at the Quality Falls trailhead.

And then there are the dinosaur tracks. Birds are descended from theropod dinosaurs, and so enjoying the Tumbler Ridge dinosaur trackways is a way of enjoying remote avian ancestral history. In summer, the Tumbler Ridge Museum Foundation conducts tours to two trackway sites: the Cabin Pool site by day and the Wolverine site by lantern-light in the evening, a uniquely evocative experience. On exhibit in the Dinosaur Discovery Gallery are some of the fossil bird trackways that have been discovered in the Tumbler Ridge area. By 2015, five such sites had already been identified, from an age spanning 40 million years, and most of the track-bearing slabs had been recovered by helicopter and added to the museum's collections. Some of these avian tracks are unlike any previously known or described. The tracks at one of these sites are among the oldest known globally, from rocks 140 million years old.

A bird checklist documenting the 240 species that have been identified in the Tumbler Ridge area is available at the visitor centre. Visitors recognize that birding in the forested foothills may be more challenging than on the prairies to the northeast, but tend to agree that a birding visit to Tumbler Ridge is unlike any other.

BIRDING GUIDE

The Bullmoose Marshes Wetland area, just off Hwy. 29, 25 km (15.5 mi.) from town, has two boardwalk trails (respectively 250 m/yd. and 650 m/yd. long). The peaceful ambience of this area makes it a favourite for local birders, especially in May and June. Summertime nesters of note include Olive-sided Flycatcher, Alder Flycatcher, Blackpoll

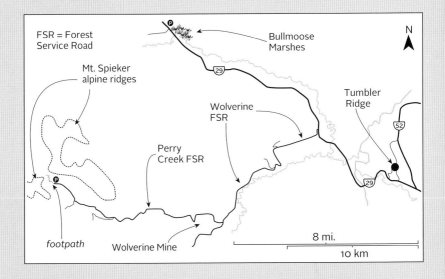

GETTING THERE

Tumbler Ridge is well signed off Hwy. 97 between Chetwynd and Dawson Creek and can be approached by either Hwy. 29 (from Chetwynd) or Hwy. 52 (from Dawson Creek). Directions to local birding areas can be found at the village information centre, but Mount Spieker is a little more complicated: From Tumbler Ridge, proceed on Hwy. 29 north toward Chetwynd/Gwillim Lake. You'll soon cross Flatbed Creek, then the larger Murray River Bridge. Zero your odometer at the bridge then drive 5.9 km (3.7 mi.) northwest before taking the exit left/west onto the Wolverine Forest Service Rd. Follow this road for 12 km (7.5 mi.), keeping the river on your left, then make a slight right onto Perry Creek Forest Service Rd. to skirt the right/north side of the old Wolverine mine. After the old mine-site, it's about 12.7 km (7.9 mi.) to the end of the road. (Stay on the main road, keeping right at two major junctions.) Park at a gas-well just below an alpine saddle. There's an obvious switch-backing trail that takes you above tree-line. From there you can turn left or right to explore either summit of Mount Spieker. Both have White-tailed and Willow Ptarmigan among other alpine specialties.

Warbler, Swamp Sparrow, and Rusty Blackbird. Watch the skies overhead for Black Swifts.

Tumbler Ridge also presents alpine access that is less challenging than in most other communities. The trail to the flat-topped summit of Mount Spieker and the hiking route up Holzworth Meadows to Ptarmigan Ridge are favourite sites, and are likely to yield both Willow and White-tailed Ptarmigan, perhaps the Timberline race of Brewer's Sparrow, and commoner alpine birds such as Horned Lark and American Pipit. Seeing Baird's Sandpiper on the high summits or enormous flocks of Lapland Longspur in the alpine in fall is a treat reserved for few birders. However, there's always the chance of seeing unexpected raptors such as Prairie Falcon. Plus, there's the Golden Eagle migration, most impressive in the fall but also discernible in spring. At the right time, an eagle may be seen speeding overhead above the alpine ridges every few minutes. A more convenient vantage point closer to town is from the pull-out off Hwy. 52 at the Quality Canyon trailhead.

◄ Bullmoose Marshes offers a great cross-section of boreal flora and fauna.
MURPHY SHEWCHUCK

The Canada Warbler is the sort of bird that takes you by surprise. More often heard than seen, the sudden appearance of such a brilliantly-coloured gem often leaves the lucky observer speechless. LIRON GERTSMAN

27

PEACE ISLAND PARK, TAYLOR

W ITH SO MANY good birding sites in the Peace River
Lowlands, it was difficult to choose which sites to
include in this book. I opted to select two areas that
are relatively compact in size, are very easy to access,
and offer a wonderful variety of Peace River specialties. The
first is Peace Island Park.

Located just off Hwy. 97 (or Mile 35 on the Alaska Hwy.)
between Dawson Creek and Fort St. John, Peace Island Park
is a popular spot for picnicking and camping. This means
it can get busy on weekends and public holidays, but there
are always plenty of quieter corners where narrow pathways
and other tracks can lead birders to some hidden gems. The
island itself is located between two back channels of the

Peace River, and is accessible by car and foot via a gravel road west of the main camping area.

Late May and all of June usually offer the best chance of catching up with breeding eastern songbirds, as they do for most of the Peace Region. Knowing your songs and calls beforehand will go a long way in helping you track down some of the common summer breeders in this park, such as Yellow-bellied Sapsucker, Least Flycatcher, Western Wood-Pewee, Red-eyed Vireo, Swainson's Thrush, Tennessee Warbler, Northern Waterthrush, Magnolia Warbler, Yellow Warbler, American Redstart, Black-and-White Warbler, White-throated Sparrow, Lincoln's Sparrow, and Baltimore Oriole. Other less common but present birds of interest include Broad-winged Hawk, Philadelphia Vireo, Eastern Phoebe, Canada Warbler, and Mourning Warbler. Also, Ruby-throated Hummingbirds occur annually in this area. There are some feeders at a private residence across the highway on Taylor Flats Sub Rd. that sometimes attract them, but they've also been spotted incidentally at this park. This is the only hummingbird species that breeds commonly in eastern North America but it's rare in the west, and this is the only area in BC where it's found. Calliope and Rufous Hummingbirds also nest in this area, with Calliope being by far the most common hummingbird overall in the area.

By July, birdsong has decreased significantly (even in the early morning), although the birds are still around. In August and September, migrant songbirds are starting to flock up and head south. Peace Island Park is wonderfully situated in the middle of a natural migration corridor: the Peace River Canyon. Most of the narrow valley is lined with

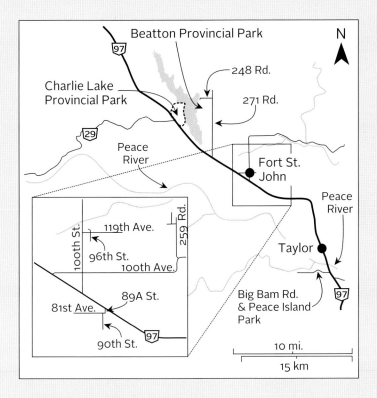

Beatton Provincial Park

97

Charlie Lake
Provincial Park

248 Rd.

271 Rd.

29

Peace
River

Fort St.
John

Peace
River

119th Ave.

259 Rd.

100th St.

96th St.

100th Ave.

Taylor

89A St.

81st Ave.

90th St.

97

Big Bam Rd.
& Peace Island
Park

97

10 mi.

15 km

GETTING THERE

Peace Island Park is well signed off the west side of Hwy. 97, immediately on the south side of the bridge over the Peace River, 20 km (12.4 mi.) south of Fort St. John or 54 km (33.6 mi.) north of Dawson Creek.

mixed shrubs and woodland, which provides good foraging habitat for a multitude of species. To the north and south are miles of relatively flat farming land, which offers little for flycatchers, vireos, and warblers. Therefore, on some days in late summer, it's easy to observe this funnelling effect as groups of warblers flit through the trees and bushes, usually heading downstream through Peace Island Park and farther east.

Winter is a quiet season for much of northern Canada, and Peace Island Park is no exception. Ruffed Grouse, American Three-toed Woodpecker, Downy Woodpecker, Hairy Wood-pecker, Pileated Woodpecker, Common Raven, Blue Jay, Black-billed Magpie, Red-breasted Nuthatch, Black-capped Chickadee, and Boreal Chickadee (the latter in patches of spruce) are some of the year-round possibilities; check the alder and birch trees for flocks of redpolls, as Hoary Redpoll is a distinct possibility in winter. Also possible here in winter, but perhaps more likely in fall and spring, is the eastern race of the White-breasted Nuthatch—a candidate to be split into a separate species from the Interior form that occurs in southern BC (pending further DNA analysis)—which favours large poplar trees.

BIRDING GUIDE

This is the kind of spot that's fairly straightforward for the visiting birder to explore. Exit off the highway, then cross the causeway onto Peace Island Park. There's a short nature trail at the west (upstream) end of the park, but it's also worth casually birding around the shrubby and forested sections at the east end and along the oxbows of the river. Big Bam Rd., the gravel road off the highway from which you enter the park, leads west to a local ski area. Walking along this road can also be great for birding as there are a few spruce trees that attract a different mix of birds, including Boreal Chickadee year-round, as well as Magnolia Warbler and the occasional Bay-breasted and Cape May Warbler in spring/summer. The alder thickets on the shaded hillside along this road are reliable for Canada Warbler in season. Knowing the songs and calls will go a long way in helping you track them down.

The squeaky-wheel song of the Black-and-White Warbler is a regular part of the dawn chorus at Beatton Provincial Park, but be wary that the ubiquitous American Redstart is a talented mimic! LIRON GERTSMAN

28

BEATTON PROVINCIAL PARK, CHARLIE LAKE

T HE ALASKA HWY., which officially begins in downtown Dawson Creek before passing through Fort St. John on its route to Fairbanks, is considered by many to be one of the greatest construction feats of the twentieth century. After the attack on Pearl Harbour in December 1941, the US government decided it needed a more efficient route to transport supplies and military personnel to Alaska. Canada agreed to allow it to pass through BC and Yukon if the Americans footed most of the bill. Construction began in February 1942; by October 1942, the 2,700 km (1,677 mi.) road was complete. During this period, Charlie Lake hosted a major camp for workers and bore witness to one of northern BC's greatest tragedies. In May 1942, a large raft carrying tractors across the lake broke apart during a storm. Despite valiant efforts by local residents, all twelve men on board died in the frigid lake water.

Fortunately, Charlie Lake is now easily accessible for anyone visiting or passing through Fort St. John on the Alaska Hwy., and offers a great mix of breeding birds during the summer months and exciting water bird migration during spring and fall. The lake is believed to have been formed by ice-damming on the Peace River many years ago, and archeological finds in some nearby caves indicate that the area has been used by various indigenous groups for around 11,000 years. Most of those early travellers were following great bison herds, whereas today it's usually fishing and summer watersports that attract people to Charlie Lake. It's a brilliant birding spot as well, of course!

Throughout the late spring and summer, large numbers of Franklin's Gulls gather on the lake each evening, with over six thousand recorded on numerous occasions. Herring, California, Mew, Ring-billed, and Bonaparte's Gulls are also common in season, but check carefully for rarer species of gulls. Arctic and Common Terns are annual, with Forster's Tern likely being rare but regular, along with the odd Parasitic Jaeger in fall.

Waterfowl numbers on the lake are generally pretty high in the April–May and September–November migration periods. Diving ducks like Surf Scoter, White-winged Scoter, Greater and Lesser Scaup, both goldeneye species, and Bufflehead are usually the most numerous, but a good number of dabblers like Mallard, Northern Pintail, and American Wigeon can number in the thousands on some days. Grebes

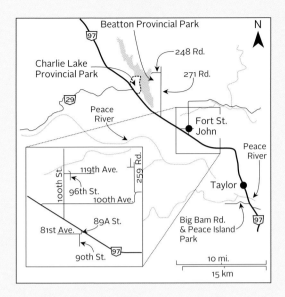

GETTING THERE

For Beatton Provincial Park, from Fort St. John, head northwest on the Alaska Hwy. in the direction of Fort Nelson. Look for signs indicating Beatton Provincial Park—a right/north turn onto 271 Rd. (3.9 km/2.4 mi. from the west end of 100th Ave. in Fort St. John). Head due north along 271 Rd. for 7.6 km (4.7 mi.) then turn left on 248 Rd., signed for Beatton Provincial Park. Follow the signs to reach the day-use area or campground, depending on your plans.

For access to the south end of Charlie Lake, return to the Alaska Hwy., and turn right (heading north) then look for an obvious turnoff to the right in 2.3 km (1.4 mi.) (Lakeshore Dr.), near an RV park and just past the well-signed Jackfish Dundee's. Park near the boat-launch and scan from a raised dyke. You can also walk the perimeter trails of Fish Creek, which can sometimes be great for marsh birds, waterfowl, and a few wading birds.

Charlie Lake Provincial Park is well signed on the east side of the Alaska Hwy., 4.5 km (2.8 mi.) north of the turnoff for the south end access and directly opposite the Hwy. 29 turnoff for Hudson's Hope.

While lakeshore and coniferous habitats are an important part of Beatton Provincial Park's birding offerings, most of the woodland here is a deciduous mix of aspen and poplar. WENDY COOMBER

and loons also use the lake during migration, and a careful eye in April or October/November might be lucky enough to spot a Yellow-billed Loon.

Three main access points to the lake offer a great variety of birding opportunities. Charlie Lake Provincial Park on the west side of the lake is largely second-growth deciduous forest with camping facilities and a boat-launch from which birders can scan the lake in the evening with the sun at their backs. The second is a boat-launch parking area at the south end of the lake that offers another opportunity for scanning. The adjacent Charlie Lake Wetland Trails, at the outflow of Fish Creek, hold potential for additional waders, ducks, and marsh birds. Finally, and most significantly, is Beatton

Provincial Park. Located on the eastern shores of Charlie Lake, it offers up a tremendous diversity of summer nesting species, including many eastern and northern specialties, and is therefore the primary focus of the following section.

BIRDING GUIDE

Beatton Provincial Park offers 330 hectares (850 acres) of mixed forest, as well as wonderful camping and picnicking facilities along a sandy beach on Charlie Lake's eastern shores. Many birders visit for a single morning, but there are enough trails here to occupy visitors for most of the day or multiple mornings. Limiting factors may be bugs (ah, northern Canada!), weather, and the time of year. The best way to beat the bugs is to come in winter when you can ski all the trails—although the birding will be a lot slower, of course!

If you're visiting in spring and summer, bring footwear that you don't mind getting wet—the trails are often overgrown with grass, which gets quite dewy in the cool mornings. Early mornings are often your best chance for spotting species like Cape May Warbler and Bay-breasted Warbler, as territorial males are more vocal and active earlier. The Peace Region tends to have a daily breeze that rolls in around 8 am and can be very frustrating if you're looking at birds in the high canopy.

If you're just making a day trip, stay left to park in the ring-shaped visitor parking area. There are plenty of birds to see along the paved roads in the park, but most of the species found in the mixed aspen woodland here will be common throughout the area. These include Western Wood-Pewee, Least Flycatcher, Red-eyed Vireo, American

Redstart, Yellow Warbler, Black-and-White Warbler, and Dark-eyed Junco. Occasionally careful eyes and ears can be rewarded though, especially in late May and early June when some birds are still on the move. In recent years, Yellow-bellied Flycatcher and Bay-breasted Warbler have been spied by birders casually strolling along the entrance road.

From the parking area, walking straight ahead will take you to the picnic area beside the beach. This is a lovely spot, but first turn left and head south across a small playing field toward a stand of tall White Spruce trees. This grove is a classic spot for Cape May Warbler and there's almost always at least one territorial male around each summer. Look and listen for them at the very top of the trees. Their high-pitched song can be confused with Black-and-White Warbler and the rarer Bay-breasted Warbler, as well as American Redstarts, which are known to mimic other warbler songs (especially Yellow, Magnolia, and Black-and-White). Black-throated Green Warblers are also present in the spruce groves in this area, often a little lower down in the trees than Cape Mays, but still frustratingly evasive when trying to get your binoculars on them. Patience and persistence are key.

Other eastern songbirds to look and listen for along these trails include Blue Jay, Blue-headed Vireo, Winter Wren, Tennessee Warbler, Ovenbird, Rose-breasted Grosbeak, White-throated Sparrow, and Baltimore Oriole. It's very interesting to see them joined by both western species such as Western Wood-Pewee and Western Tanager, as well as northern residents such as Spruce Grouse, American Three-toed Woodpecker, Gray Jay, Boreal Chickadee, and White-winged Crossbill. Numbers of these latter species may fluctuate depending on cone crops and other food sources, but any visit in summer should yield an interesting mix of birds that is fairly unique to this region.

After satisfying your lust for eastern warblers, or simply becoming fed up with high-pitched call notes and mosquitos, return to the playing field and walk down to the waterfront. Eastern Phoebes often nest in the picnic shelter and can be heard calling from their insect-hawking perches along the lakeshore. Spotted Sandpipers are often bobbing along the beach in spring and summer, while Lincoln's and Song Sparrows give their songs from nearby shrubs. It's always worth setting up a scope to scan the lake here. As mentioned previously, Franklin's Gulls are often seen in large numbers on Charlie Lake. Evening is best as they often clear out early in the morning, but scattered flocks can be seen throughout the day from this area. In migration, large numbers of Black Terns are occasionally seen on the lake, along with lesser numbers of Common and Arctic Terns. Rarer but likely annual are Forster's and Caspian Terns. Identification of the smaller white terns can be very difficult, so take good notes of the features you can observe and compare them to descriptions in your field guide.

Outside of mid-summer, as long as the lake isn't frozen, there's usually a good variety of waterfowl out on the lake. A good scope is often necessary as it's a large lake with limited access points. September–November is the period with the most potential for rarities like jaegers and Yellow-billed Loon. For map, see page 185.

Liard River Hot Springs is close to the western limit for many eastern species, including the Rose-breasted Grosbeak. Their sweet warbling song can be heard from great distance, and is often given from high in an aspen or poplar.

LIRON GERTSMAN

29

LIARD RIVER
HOT SPRINGS,
ALASKA HIGHWAY

AFTER A LONG day on the Alaska Hwy., whether you're travelling from Fort Nelson or Yukon, there's no better place to take a break than the Liard River Hot Springs. Open year-round to the public, with camping available May 1–September 30, visitors will fall in love with these natural hot pools, surrounded by lush, almost jungle-like vegetation in summer and charming snowscapes in winter.

I should also mention that this is a fantastic stop for birding as well! The hot springs' location in the North Rockies is a continuation of the "East meets West" theme mentioned in Tumbler Ridge (see page 169). Both MacGillivray's and

Mourning Warblers are common here, providing the clearest example of this, but you may also note eastern birds like Yellow-bellied Sapsucker, Blue-headed Vireo, Philadelphia Vireo, Winter Wren, and Baltimore Oriole mingling with western species like Pacific Wren, Western Wood-Pewee, Hammond's Flycatcher, Townsend's Warbler, and Western Tanager. As this is the western edge for some of these eastern birds, their numbers will fluctuate each year, with birds like Baltimore Oriole and Philadelphia Vireo being absent at times and common at others. Mew Gulls nest in the nearby marsh, and northern specialists like Boreal Owl, Northern Hawk-Owl, Boreal Chickadee, Gray Jay, and Rusty Blackbird all breed in the area.

Larger wildlife such as moose and wood bison are common as well. Enjoy these delights, but give them space! This location is no secret, but the pools are large enough that you rarely feel crowded and there are ample trails and boardwalks for birders to spread out and explore. The only problem will be keeping your bins from fogging up!

BIRDING GUIDE

This park is relatively small, so birding is fairly straightforward. Early morning is the best time for birdsong and will also help you avoid the main crowds. If you're able to plan ahead, early to mid-June is the best time to find breeding birds in this area, as the males become less vocal by July.

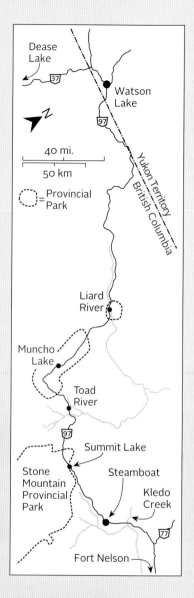

GETTING THERE

Liard River Hot Springs Provincial Park is well signed just off the Alaska Hwy. (97), 300 km (186 mi.) west of Fort Nelson and 206 km (128 mi.) east of Watson Lake, Yukon.

All three ptarmigan species occur in the Haines Triangle, but Willow Ptarmigan (pictured) are by far the most abundant species close to the highway. If visiting in early summer, be sure to hang around until evening when the males put on spectacular clucking flight displays. ILYA POVALYAEV

30

HAINES TRIANGLE, NORTHWESTERN BC

IT MUST HAVE been July 3, 2010, when I rolled into Whitehorse with fellow birders Ian Cruickshank of Victoria and Chris Coxson of Prince George after a long drive across Yukon. I was doing a "big year" (trying to see as many species as possible in BC in one calendar year). We stayed the night at my Uncle Syd's place and had a great get-together with other Yukon birders like Cameron Eckert, Jukka Jantunen, and Ted Murphy-Kelly, picking their brains about the birds of the Haines Triangle. The next day we woke early to drive out to Haines Junction, Yukon. When we pulled into the Fas Gas there, a young Native woman walked up to me and asked, "Are you Russell Cannings?" My mind scrambled to understand how she could possibly know who I was.

Had my blog suddenly become a cult classic in Haines Junction? Had word spread throughout the bird-world that "the big year guy" might possibly be passing through Haines Junction and this #1 fan had been waiting for weeks just to see me???

"Your uncle just called. He said you forgot all your food in Whitehorse."

"Oh…"

Well, at least Haines Junction has a "General Store" which gave us enough to last for a couple days in the wilds of the Haines Triangle. We headed due south on the road to Haines, Alaska, and passed back into BC around lunchtime. We weren't surprised to see storm clouds on the horizon, nor were we psyched out by the wind. Here was a triangle, bordered on two sides by Alaska. With nesting species like Gyrfalcon, Gray-cheeked Thrush, American Tree Sparrow, Common Redpoll, and Smith's Longspur, it almost shouldn't be in BC at all, but we weren't complaining. For the three of us it was a mysterious slice of the north with enticing possibilities, and nothing short of a grizzly bear would dissuade us from our avian aspirations.

BIRDING GUIDE

It's almost exactly 100 km (62 mi.) to the BC border from Haines Junction (Yukon Hwy. 3, also known as the Haines Hwy.). On the drive south, you pass two large lakes: Kathleen Lake to the west and Dezadeash Lake to the east. Once in BC, you've made it to the fabled Haines Triangle. From the BC–Yukon border, the now-paved Haines Rd. slowly climbs up the Tatshenshini River Valley, across Datlasaka

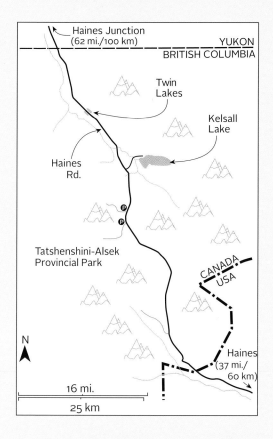

GETTING THERE

The BC section of the paved Haines Rd. between Haines Junction, YT, and Haines, AK, is about 73 km (45 mi.) long and takes around an hour to drive without stopping. You can drive or fly into White-horse; then it's a 3.5-hour drive to the BC border. Alternatively, Haines, AK, has car-ferry services from all the main Alaska ports as well as Prince Rupert, Port Hardy, and Bellingham, Washington, among others. There are no services or accommodations in the Haines Triangle (BC section) so it's advisable to carry extra fuel, appropriate camping gear, and plenty of food. As always, be on the lookout for bears, always carry bear spray, and never hike off the road alone. If possible, tell somewhere what your plans are before leaving cell range.

The Haines Triangle is home to several breeding species more normally associated with the Yukon and Alaska. Among them is the world's largest falcon: the Gyrfalcon. This one was hunting Arctic Ground Squirrels on the side of the road. RUSSELL CANNINGS

and Mosquito Flats (covered in boggy fens and willow scrub), then up and over the Chilkat Pass, and down the Klehini River to the border with Alaska. Summer is generally the best time to visit, as the weather is optimal and the birds abundant. Birdsong peaks in June, but many of the summer breeders can still be seen in July and August.

The Twin Lakes (signed), 14 km (8.7 mi.) south of the Yukon border, are worth checking out. Arctic Terns can usually be observed in high numbers during the summer, with a few Bonaparte's, Mew, and Herring Gulls mixed in. American Wigeon, Lesser Yellowlegs, Wilson's Snipe, Gray-cheeked Thrush, Common Yellowthroat, and possibly Greater Scaup and Short-billed Dowitcher all breed in this area.

The access road (an unmarked dirt road) to Kelsall Lake is sometimes a little tricky to see, but you should be able to find it on the east side, about 12 km (7.5 mi.) south of the Twin Lakes. It's often impossible to drive all the way to the lake because of washouts, but it's only a 3.5 km (2.2 mi.) hike from the road in flat although sometimes wet terrain. The willows here are loaded with Willow Ptarmigan, Wilson's Warbler, American Tree Sparrow, Golden-crowned Sparrow, Fox Sparrow, and Common Redpoll; the wetlands can yield Wilson's Snipe, Lesser Yellowlegs, and Least Sandpiper. Smith's Longspurs were regular nesters in this area until the late 1980s, but smaller snowpacks in winter have resulted in increased willow growth along the road, which is not to these birds' liking. They can likely be found farther up in the hills where the willows are more spaced out and stunted (about waist-height)—but that requires birders to go and look! The lake itself can be quiet in summer, but you never know what you might find. May and September are the best times for birders.

Note: *Be extremely wary of Grizzly Bears, especially if you're hiking away from the main road. This area supports a healthy population, and they can easily be hidden in the dense willows. If you plan to venture away from the road, inform others of your intentions and try not to go alone. Carry bear spray and make lots of noise when passing through thick patches of willows.

Continuing along Haines Rd., you'll pass several hiking trailheads on the west side of the road—some are short and some longer, but all follow creeks uphill into Tatshenshini-Alsek Provincial Park. Once you clear the willow scrub, it's easy to hike around the tundra at the base of the St. Elias Mountains. It's a good idea to bring a map and a GPS along—when you lose sight of the main road it's easy to get confused by the abundance of small lakes and rivers. Once out of the willows, look for Semipalmated Plover, American Pipit, and Horned Lark in the mossy tundra. Wandering Tattlers are fairly common around the small lakes and shingle rivers. Hike up Stonehouse Creek (signed off Haines Rd.) for one of the quickest ways into their preferred habitat (hike about 1 km/0.6 mi. into the tundra habitat, then choose which lakes/ridges to explore). Arctic Tern, Herring Gull, and Mew Gull all breed around these lakes, as well as Least Sandpiper and Savannah Sparrow. Snow Buntings have been recorded in the rocky slopes above, and perhaps an intrepid birder will one day confirm Northern Wheatear from those high rocky ridges. Both Rock and White-tailed Ptarmigan are possible in the high country, and Gyrfalcon and Golden Eagle nest on the cliffs.

Back on the main road, after the impressive Three Guardsmen peaks, the road starts to descend swiftly south toward Haines, Alaska. Just before the border, habitat along the roadside will take on the distinctly "coastal" feel of Western Hemlock and Sitka Spruce forest. Sooty Grouse, Red-breasted Sapsucker, and Chestnut-backed Chickadee are some of the coastal birds to be expected here.

INDEX

ABOUT THE AUTHORS

Russell Cannings has been an avid birder since his childhood in BC's Okanagan. He has worked extensively as a field biologist throughout the province. However since completing a History degree at UBC and an Education degree at Vancouver Island University, he has relocated to New Zealand's North Island to start a new adventure as a high-school teacher.

Richard Cannings is a veteran biologist, birder, and nature writer. A lifetime resident of BC's Okanagan Valley, he is a founding director of the Okanagan Similkameen Conservation Alliance and a member of the national board of the Nature Conservancy of Canada. He is the author of several books, including *British Columbia: A Natural History of Its Origins, Ecology, and Diversity with a New Look at Climate Change* and *The New B.C. Roadside Naturalist: A Guide to Nature along B.C. Highways.*